"Sicile-Kira and her autistic son, Jeremy, join forces in this guidebook to help parents and their autistic offspring move beyond childhood and evolve into an adult life. . . . The author breaks each large, seemingly overwhelming undertaking into small, doable tasks. . . . A proactive method for raising an adult child with special needs."

—*Kirkus Reviews*

"If you are raising a teen with significant autistic challenges, you need to read *A Full Life with Autism*. If you have a young child who is nonverbal, you need to read *A Full Life with Autism*. Chantal Sikle-Kira's newest book is co-authored with her son Jeremy, who did not speak, but who writes eloquently and powerfully. The mother-son dialogue, facilitated by keyboard and iPad, is a striking example of the potential inside many nonverbal people. Together, they walk the reader through the challenges of leaving home and establishing an independent life as an adult. The step-by-step manner in which they do this, and Jeremy's calm and steady voice, will be very reassuring to readers. Topics discussed include making friends, romance, housing, college, and finally, earning a living. I particularly like the way this book weaves both Chantal and Jeremy's perspective into each story. In the latter part of the book, some chapters are also illustrated with stories from other families. This is a very practical guide that I highly recommend."

—John Elder Robison, author of *Look Me in the Eye* and *Be Different*

"This truly impressive book by Chantal Sicile-Kira and her son Jeremy, who is in his early twenties and autistic, will serve as an invaluable resource not only for families who have a youngster or young adult with autism but also for the professionals who work with these families. *A Full Life with Autism* vividly brings to life not only the challenges and stresses faced by young adolescents and adults on the autism spectrum but also steps that can be taken to assist these individuals to become more independent, successful, and resilient."

—Robert Brooks, PhD, Faculty, Harvard Medical School, and coauthor of *Raising Resilient Children with Autism Spectrum Disorders* and *The Power of Resilience*

"*A Full Life with Autism* provides a timely and compelling perspective into the struggles and challenges of adults with autism and their caregivers. Chantal and Jeremy accurately portray so many of the issues that young adults experience as they move into the world and seek to find their voice and purpose. *A Full Life with Autism* is certain to be an important resource for young adults and their families trying to understand, cope, and thrive during one of the most important transitions for an individual with autism."

> —Areva D. Martin, Esq., Managing Partner, Martin
> & Martin, LLP; president, Special Needs Network,
> Inc.; and author, *The Everyday Advocate: Standing Up
> for Your Child with Autism or Other Special Needs*

"Chantal Sicile-Kira and the remarkable (once considered 'retarded') Jeremy Sicile-Kira have created a work wherein their common goal is obvious: Separation, and independence for Jeremy. Their writing is filled with a refreshing respect for one another, and very often the material is quite brave."

> —Michael John Carley, executive director, GRASP,
> ASTEP, and author of *Asperger's From the Inside-Out*

"For individuals with autism what we 'see' rarely tells us what each is thinking, feeling, or capable of accomplishing. We must look beyond the 'behaviors' to understand what each is trying to communicate. *A Full Life with Autism* does this and so much more. Truly a must-read!"

> —Ricki G. Robinson, MD, MPH, member, Scientific Review
> Panel of Autism Speaks, and author of *Autism Solutions: How
> to Create a Healthy and Meaningful Life for Your Child*

"*A Full Life with Autism* is a must-read book for parents and professionals in the autism field."

> —Steve Edelson, PhD, director, Autism Research Institute

"A full life can have many different meanings for many different people, and yet, on a deeper level, when we hear the phrase 'full life' we seem to become united by a common human objective we would not wish to deny ourselves or others. In this important book, Jeremy and Chantal Sicile-Kira have captured the value of our shared humanity within our diversity. They do this gracefully, leading the way, as the next generation of young people with autism seek their paths."

> —Valerie Paradiz, PhD, director, Autistic Global
> Initiative, Autism Research Institute

"Unfortunately, many adults on the autism experience have high rates of un-employment or underemployment. Some of our most gifted live in poverty and have few options in life. Chantal and Jeremy have creatively worked to create an engaged life for Jeremy and his family. This book provides very practical ideas for transition planning and provides a template that others can use as they support adults moving into adulthood. I highly recommend this for any family or individual as they prepare for transition planning."
—Dr. Cathy Pratt, director, Indiana Resource Center for Autism

"This book will help us all navigate the new world of employment for persons on the autistic spectrum."
—Michael Bernick, former director, California Labor Department, and autism employment activist

"*A Full Life with Autism* is an important book that should be on the shelf of all schools, therapists, parents, and caregivers serving individuals with an autism spectrum diagnosis. . . . Jeremy is living proof that respect and support are key to an individual with an ASD diagnosis living a full life. In this book, Jeremy gives the reader valuable insights into the mind of the nonverbal, significantly impacted individual with ASD, and Jeremy and Chantal both give practical tips and directions to parents, caregivers, and others for major facets of life integral to living a fulfilling life as an adult with autism."
—Teri Arranga, director, AutismOne, and editor-in-chief, *Autism Science Digest*

"The transition into adult life is poorly understood and seldom researched in the field of autism. Jeremy and Chantal Sicile-Kira have given us important lessons from their knowledge and experience. They write honestly and clearly and their book will be of great benefit to the thousands of other families who wish to support their loved one with dignity and respect."
—Anne M. Donnellan, professor, University of San Diego, and professor emerita, University of Wisconsin-Madison

"I have a new favorite book about autism! Chantal Sicile-Kira has clearly done her homework in addressing issues for young adults with autism and their parents. But having parallel comments and suggestions from her son Jer-emy adds a deeper perspective and value to an already excellent book. I will be returning to this book. The dual voices of parent advocate and self-advocate, commenting in parallel on the same topics, are a revelation to read."
—Scott Standifer, Disability Policy & Studies, University of Missouri School of Health Professions

"This is a highly readable book. Chantal and Jeremy Sicile-Kira succeed in addressing how each individual on the spectrum is unique and will need personally tailored supports."

—Lars Perner, PhD, assistant professor of Clinical Marketing, University of Southern California, and chair, Panel of People on the Spectrum of Autism Advisors, Autism Society of America

A Full Life with Autism lays out in plain language the challenges of transition to adulthood for persons with autism. This book belongs on the shelf, e-player, or e-reader of everyone who strives to help people with autism and ASDs."

—Joshua Feder, MD, Director of Research of the Interdisciplinary Council on Developmental and Learning Disorders

"If you are a parent of a person with autism or a professional in this area, you will find that you will refer to the book over and over again. It is both timely and timeless."

—Dr. Donald N. Cardinal, dean of the College of Educational Studies at Chapman University

"Chantal Sicile-Kira and her son Jeremy guide us on a journey that an ever-increasing number of families are confronting as adolescents on the spectrum transition to young adulthood. With insight and candor, underscored by Chantal's extensive efforts in the field, they outline the options that are available and offer wide-ranging guidance to those on this journey."

—Barbara Firestone, PhD, president and CEO, The Help Group; and Louis Vismara, MD, Board Chair, The MIND Institute

"Although written for parents of transition-age youth, this book has the invaluable perspective of those living with autism that is of interest to all families and professionals dedicated to individuals with autism spectrum disorders. Reading this book I felt as if I was experiencing the challenges to realize the goals and dreams associated with becoming a young adult along with Jeremy and Chantal Sicile-Kira."

—Laura J. Hall, professor, Department of Special Education San Diego State University

A FULL LIFE
WITH AUTISM

From Learning
to Forming Relationships
to Achieving Independence

Chantal Sicile-Kira
and
Jeremy Sicile-Kira

palgrave
macmillan

First published in 2012 by PALGRAVE MACMILLAN® in the
U.S.—a division of St. Martin's Press LLC, 175 Fifth Avenue, New
York, NY 10010.

Where this book is distributed in the UK, Europe, and the rest of
the world, this is by Palgrave Macmillan, a division of Macmillan
Publishers Limited, registered in England, company number 785998,
of Houndmills, Basingstoke, Hampshire RG21 6XS.

Palgrave Macmillan is the global academic imprint of the above
companies and has companies and representatives throughout the
world.

Palgrave® and Macmillan® are registered trademarks in the United
States, the United Kingdom, Europe, and other countries.

ISBN: 978-0-230-11246-9

Library of Congress Cataloging-in-Publication Data
Sicile-Kira, Chantal.
    A full life with autism : from learning to forming relationships to
achieving independence / Chantal Sicile-Kira, Jeremy Sicile-Kira.
        p. cm.
    Includes bibliographical references and index.
    ISBN 978-0-230-11246-9 (pbk.)
    1. Autism—Popular works. 2. Autism—Age factors—Popular
works. 3. Life skills. I. Sicile-Kira, Jeremy. II. Title.
RC553.A88S5665 2012
616.85882—dc23
                                                            2011038738

A catalogue record of the book is available from the British Library.

Design by Letra Libre

First edition: March 2012

10 9 8 7 6 5 4 3 2 1

Printed in the United States of America.

For Maman,

*and for all the Rosa Parkses
who have been paving the way*

for those with autism and their families.

—Chantal

To my family.

—Jeremy

The potential of people with autism to live in the community, to engage in the community, to enjoy life in the community is really as limitless as the potential for anyone else to do so. None of us are asking for guarantees. What we are asking for is an avenue by which there [are] equal opportunities to access those things that help define an individual's quality of life.

—Peter Gerhardt, Ed.D., President, Organization for Autism Research (Advancing Futures for Adults with Autism, Congressional Briefing Report, www.afaa-us.org)

Too often autistic children are raised to believe they are broken and need to be fixed. Adults with autism too often live lives of isolation and poverty. Understanding people's experiences may lead to acceptance, accommodation and appropriate support. To continue down the same paths, well-worn for 65 years, when all these data impel us to rethink our assumptions and broaden our path is unthinkable.

—Anne Donellan, Ph.D., Martha Leary, MA CCC-LP, "Rethinking Autism: Implications of Sensory and Movement Differences," *Disability Studies Quarterly*

CONTENTS

ACKNOWLEDGMENTS

JEREMY:

My future is dependent on others. Justly I thank all my wonderful support staff and therapists, past and present. Special thanks to Soma Mukhopadhyay, who provided a way for me to learn and communicate. I am most grateful to Bruce Cochrane for believing in me; Allan Gustafson for recognizing my abilities; Darlene Hanson and Mary Jane Palmer for helping with my communication skills; Michelle Hardy for helping me gain more control of my body; Dr. Carl Hillier and his great team for helping me to really see; and Nancy Brady for frankly making inclusion possible. Thanks to all the Afternoon Angels and my Team Jeremy, past and present, for being such an important influence in my life. Realize the major role you have played in my being the person that I am today. Thanks to my nice agent Lindsay Edgecombe and editor Luba Ostashevsky for giving me the opportunity to write this book. I want to thank Blaze Ginsberg for being a good friend. Thanks to my dog, Handsome, for his loyalty. My mom has the most patience and kindly she has given me much hope. Nice thanks to Daniel and Rebecca for their love.

CHANTAL:

Once again, I am grateful to James Levine and Lindsay Edgecombe for their assistance and encouragement in developing the idea Jeremy and I had that finally became a manuscript. The wise advice of Luba Ostashevsky, our fearless editor, was useful and much appreciated, and has made this book a better read. Many thanks to Christopher Johnson for his creative talent and patience. I am indebted to Temple Grandin, who is so generous of her time and insight. Thanks to all who shared their research and their personal stories so that we could better inform readers. As always, I am extremely grateful to the current Team Jeremy as well as to the Afternoon Angels and all educators, therapists, and paraprofessionals from past years. Without the support of all of you, Jeremy would not be the young man he is today. Much love and thanks to Daniel, Jeremy, and Rebecca, as always. Finally, kudos to Jeremy for having the courage to share his story in order to help others.

FOREWORD

O ne of the most difficult times for many individuals on the autism spectrum is making the transition into adulthood. This is an area that is sadly neglected despite the fact that it is hugely important. I have had teachers and parents tell me many sad stories in which a young adult loses a job or drops out of college because they were not prepared for a world away from home. Sometimes they lack the most basic skills, such as getting up on time or being late for class. Before I went to college, I had basic skills such as driving, handling a checking account, shopping, and doing laundry. Too often parents coddle their children and do these chores for them instead of teaching them how to do them themselves. Too often students leave high school or transition programs unready for the realities of life as an adult.

This book will greatly help parents prepare for what lies ahead and know what their sons and daughters need to learn. Jeremy and Chantal each write from their own perspective and share practical information about different areas of life that can be difficult to navigate, including housing, employment, college, as well as social relationships.

One basic principle in working with individuals on the autism spectrum is "no surprises." Surprises cause panic and fear. The individual needs to know what the new place will be like BEFORE they go there. A college or a job site should be

visited before the individual starts work or school. If this is
not possible, then he/she should see lots of photos, websites,
or talk to some of the people in the new place.

GRADUAL TRANSITION

I made a gradual transition from the world of school to work.
When I was thirteen years old, Mother arranged a job for me
hand-sewing hems for a freelance seamstress. When I was fifteen, I took care of nine horses and built a gate on my aunt's
ranch that could be opened from a car. I was often reluctant to
try new things, but Mother always gave me a choice. I could
try it for a week and if I hated it, I did not have to stay. It was
important for my development that I was always encouraged
to try new things. Even though I was originally afraid to go to
the ranch, I loved it after I got there. When I was in graduate
school, I was writing a column for the *Arizona Farmer Ranch-
man* and painting signs at the state fair. I think it is essential
to get work experiences while the child is in high school. They
need to learn how to do tasks that other people want. Jeremy is
very impacted by his autism, yet during high school he learned
work skills with the help of his teacher and mother, who created two self-employment ventures based on services people
needed on campus. Good jobs for teenagers are dog walking,
fixing computers, writing for a community newsletter, or making and selling greeting cards.

When I was in college, I did an internship at a research
lab and worked at a program for autistic children. When I did
the research lab internship, I rented a house with another lady.
The house rental with the other person was arranged through
people at the lab. To succeed, individuals at all levels on the
spectrum need to be "stretched." The principle is to "stretch"
the individual but not cause panic by pushing too hard. However, if you never "stretch," then there will be no advancement.
It is never too late to start working with the individual. Even if

he/she is thirty years old and sits in the basement playing video games all day, he/she can still try new things. A person on the spectrum always keeps learning. I'm sixty-four years old and I learn something new every day.

Temple Grandin, author of
Thinking in Pictures and
The Way I See It
August 2011

PREFACE

*By refusing to give in to despair, I have the power to believe that
I will conquer all obstacles to live a normal life.*

—Jeremy

CHANTAL:

Since the publication of my books *Adolescents on the Autism
Spectrum* and *Autism Life Skills,* and Jeremy's appearance on
MTV's *True Life: I Have Autism,* we've received many emails
from parents and educators asking for advice. While Jeremy was
heading toward graduation from high school and transitioning
into adulthood, they wanted to know what life was like for him
and what his plans were for the future. I was being asked what I
was doing to help Jeremy and about the resources available. The
number of teenagers on the autism spectrum who will soon be
aging out of the school system is estimated at between 700,000
and 800,000. We wanted to share what information we had in
order to help others navigating this major life transition.

This book offers advice from different perspectives. It reflects Jeremy's dreams and goals and the challenges he's overcoming to meet them. Then it explains how we create that
life with the assistance of the adult services for those with

developmental disabilities when possible, and designing our own solutions when necessary. As well, we have included current research and resources useful to parents and educators of young adults on the autism spectrum of all different ability levels. The last few years of high school, Jeremy was very clear about what kind of life he planned on having as an adult. I felt that as his mother it was my responsibility to help him reach his goals. It is important to note that Jeremy has the same dreams as his neurotypical sister, Rebecca, who graduated from high school the same year he did. Jeremy wants to go to college, live in his own place, get married, earn a living doing what he likes to do, and give back to his community. And I don't see why he should aspire to anything less than that.

When Jeremy was born and subsequently diagnosed, I was told to find a good institution for him. The medical expert who advised me to do that had no idea that I had a background in autism. As an assistant recreation therapist at a California state hospital, I helped a group of young people with autism prepare for deinstitutionalization. I helped people get out of institutions; placing my son in one was never an option. In fact, many challenging years later, we like to joke that we have found the perfect institution for Jeremy—it's called "college."

Both parents and educators of children with disabilities are familiar with special education services, which, although not perfect, have seen tremendous improvement when it comes to educating children with autism. In the United States, all children are guaranteed FAPE—a Free and Appropriate Public Education—under the Individuals with Disabilities in Education Act (IDEA). IDEA is a federal law that governs how early intervention, special education, and related services are provided to children with disabilities, from birth through at least twenty-one years of age (some states provide educational services until age twenty-two, or even twenty-five). In school, each child is provided with an Individual Education Program (IEP), developed by a team of educators and parents for that student. Parents and educators may argue about what is meant by "fair and appropriate," but clearly there are laws protecting our children's rights to an education. As well, the knowledge base of how to best educate children with autism spectrum disorders of different abilities has steadily improved over the years.

When students reach the age of sixteen (in some states sooner), an Individual Transition Plan (ITP) must be developed along with the IEP. The ITP outlines transition goals and services for the student, mapping out long-term adult outcomes from which annual goals and objectives are defined. The purpose is to prepare the student for adult life while he or she is still under the auspices of school services provided under IDEA. However, there is no federal law mandating that services be provided once a person has aged out or graduated from the school system. Parents who have skillfully negotiated the special education maze are often surprised and discouraged by the lack of supports, adult programs, or options provided when their young adult ages out of special education services.

Despite the years of discussion, planning, and careful preparation, the transition to adult services for Jeremy has not been smooth. Jeremy had an effective and well-thought-out transition program provided by the school district until he turned twenty-two. However, the adult services in place are not prepared for providing programs or supports for those on the spectrum of different abilities. The state of the economy and budget cuts do not help, but the problems run much deeper than that. Research conducted while writing this book sadly confirmed that this is the case almost everywhere. I've heard and read many heart-wrenching stories from around the country about adults leaving school and then being unable to find or keep a job, or finish college. It is important to recognize that it is the systems charged with teaching the appropriate adult living and working skills and providing job opportunities that are failing, not our adult children.

The adult services in place need to recognize that not everyone on the spectrum is the same and that their needs and abilities are different. It also requires that all of us parents, professionals, and organizations do what we can to create the changes we want to see.

If parents and educators have learned anything over the years, it is that the label of autism means nothing, and yet it means everything. Autism is like the elephant in the Indian parable of the blind men and the elephant. A group of blind men feel a different part of an elephant and then compare notes. Each has a different opinion of what the elephant is, depending on which part of the elephant they explored. Such is autism. Our experiences are different because our children present different strengths and challenges.

ABOUT THIS BOOK

Jeremy is creating his adult life, and we are on a clear path and very optimistic about his future. We hope our experiences shared in this book will be helpful and inspirational to the reader. I believe that forewarned is forearmed, and in that spirit we have shared some of our frustrations as well as our positive experiences. Keep in mind that just as there are differences in the quality and choice of education provided from school district to school district governed by the same laws, there are differences in adult services from one city to another, and from state to state.

Although Jeremy's journey into adulthood is the premise of this book, we have covered the spectrum of ability levels by sharing the experiences of individuals of a variety of abilities as well as resources you can turn to for more information. This book is by no means a complete review of all the resources that exist. Rather, it is a guidebook that will give readers creative ideas as well as referrals to organizations and literature to help launch your loved one's journey into adult life.

To create the future that you and your adult child envision will take perseverance and work. But good quality of life and peace of mind is worth it. There are many like-minded parents and caring professionals out there. Together we can build upon what was started by those before us, and continue to build a future of possibilities.

JEREMY:

My education at Torrey Pines High School has been my greatest achievement. I was once considered autistic and severely retarded. In 2010, at age twenty-one, I graduated from high school with a full academic diploma and a GPA of 3.78. I am continuing my education by taking classes at the local community college. I want to transfer to a four-year college, major in communications, and graduate. I hope to learn how to communicate my ideas effectively in order to become a better advocate for the autism community as well as a friend to others.

My story is like Helen Keller's, the amazing woman who started out deaf, mute, and blind. Helen Keller had a teacher, Anne Sullivan, who taught her and took her out of isolation. When Helen Keller grew up, she graduated from college, became an author, and advocated for people with disabilities. Like Helen Keller I am on a similar path.

People tell me that I am a good example of overcoming challenges and never giving up. When I was a baby, I was not able to move very much because I had hypotonia—very low muscle tone. I had lots of physical therapy. It was also hard to use any of my senses. Little by little my mom gave me the tools to recognize that everything had meaning. She read to me often and made me understand the connection between words and images and sound. My mom frankly did not try to treat me differently than she would have if I had been neurotypical. She talked to me as if I understood everything.

Still, I had no appropriate way of communicating. I had auditory integration therapy to help me process what I was hearing when

I was four or five. Much later, I had vision therapy that helped with my vision processing. When I was five, my mom and students she hired used Applied Behavior Analysis (ABA—a method that shapes behavior through rewards and prompts) to teach me, and in this way they reached me. Later, it was the Rapid Prompting Method (RPM) that really opened up a world of possibilities for me. RPM uses a "teach and ask" paradigm for eliciting responses through intensive verbal, visual, and/or tactile prompts. It is a way to teach academics that leads to communication through typing.

My mom saved me from a life of despair, much like Anne Sullivan did for Helen Keller, and then many good teachers followed in Mom's footsteps. Now I am able to take college-level academic classes. I communicate and do my coursework through the use of an iPad with voice-output technology. I present at conferences about autism and write to create awareness and to help parents understand their nonverbal children. I developed an interest in becoming an advocate for people with autism after my appearance on MTV's True Life: I Have Autism. *Viewers wrote to tell me that they were inspired by how I found a way to communicate despite the fact that I am nonverbal and have many other challenges. Since last year I have been a staff writer on my college newspaper. It makes me feel good to learn that neurotypical people are interested in my experiences and how I see the world.*

Neurotypicals might think people with autism are all the same. I have to disagree. Unfortunately, most neurotypical people are misinformed about autism unless they have been exposed to it as either a relative or an educator. The rest get their information and base their beliefs on what they see in the media. The way people with autism are portrayed on TV or in movies is usually based on a few extraordinary individuals and is not a good representation of the autism community as a whole.

Many neurotypicals make assumptions about self-stimulatory behavior (the rocking, the flapping of hands, and stimming with a small item). When people first meet me and see my self-stimulatory behaviors, they assume I am unintelligent or mentally retarded.

Then they see me type, or they read an article I have written. If a person were to read anything I wrote before they met me, I think their judgment would be very different than if they met me in person first.

All of us on the spectrum are different from one another, and our wants and hopes are as well. It is important to recognize that when planning our lives. Mighty systems are in place that don't understand this. Our nation was built on the principle that all people are created equally, yet all Americans are not treated equally. African Americans, women, gay people, and the disabled continue to struggle, even those who have been given equal rights. Systemic change will not happen unless we convince society that we are all differently abled yet deserve equal consideration.

My life will not always be easy, but I believe that with all the great and caring professionals and support staff I have been lucky enough to meet, I will have a wonderful, interesting, and productive life. Hopefully, I will make more friends.

NOTES ABOUT
THE BOOK

We have tried to use terminology that is people first, encompassing, and nonjudgmental throughout the book when referring to individuals on the autism spectrum. In cases discussing someone we know, we used their preferred terminology (i.e., autistic, Asperger's, High Functioning Autism). We have used the terms *ASD* (Autism Spectrum Disorders) and *on the spectrum* to refer to anyone with autism or Asperger's Syndrome. *Aspie,* when used, refers to a person with Asperger's Syndrome.

Mostly we have used the pronoun *he,* sometimes *she,* but the information here, unless otherwise noted, is applicable to all genders.

We have used the term *parent,* but we realize that grandparents, other relatives, guardians, and caretakers are raising youths with autism, and we include them in the term *parent.*

In most cases, we have changed the names of people as we relate their experiences in order to protect their privacy.

Please note that the information in this book is the personal opinion of the authors. None of the advice in this book is to be considered legal, medical, or therapeutic advice. For any decisions considering those areas, please contact your trusted medical professional, therapist, or attorney and seek their professional advice.

CHAPTER 1

TRANSITIONING OUR YOUNG ADULT, TRANSITIONING OURSELVES

Rome was not built in a day. I need time to build the Eiffel Tower that my life will become.

—Jeremy

Jeremy's educational experience has run the gamut from typical nursery schools in Europe, to behavior-based home programs, to special education and general education classrooms in the United States. Over the years he learned to say simple three-word sentences—such as "I want ..."—but could not verbalize more than three or four syllables at a time due to motor challenges. When Jeremy entered his local high school, at age fourteen, he was placed in a classroom for the severely handicapped. He began to learn to spell and type at home, and he eventually attended general education classes. Jeremy had a paraprofessional aide and received both occupational therapy services and speech therapy. When he was twenty, he passed the CAH-SEE, the California High School Exit Exam—a requirement in this state at the time—along with passing a certain number of units, and he graduated with a full academic diploma in June 2010 at the age of twenty-one.

The high school district continued to provide services until the semester he turned twenty-two, in January 2011, as it was decided that he was not ready to transition out of school services at that time. While Jeremy was in his last semester of high school, he took his first community college class, and the school district was an enormous support for this transition. Well aware of Jeremy's needs as well as his goals in life, we had started discussions years earlier with his case manager at our local Regional Center about adult services for Jeremy. Regional Centers are contracted with the Department of Developmental Services in California to help plan, access, coordinate, and monitor services and supports to individuals with developmental disabilities. Adult services include (in theory) day programs, work services programs, some education services, and assistance with different types of housing options.

For years I was told, "Don't worry. We understand Jeremy's needs. We'll figure it out." When the first wave of budget cuts became reality a few years back, the case manager and I started to panic, but then I was told there were some creative options that were working for others, and perhaps they would work for Jeremy. The Regional Center case manager had been present at most of his IEP meetings over the years, so they were aware of Jeremy's need for a one-to-one support person and of his goals of getting a four-year degree in communications, becoming a writer, and becoming an advocate for those with autism. Jeremy's plan is to eventually earn enough money to pay for the cost of the support person he needs in order to work. After graduating from high school while attending community college part-time, he became a staff writer on the community college newspaper, had some opportunities to earn money through writing, and was invited to present at autism conferences—which is to say, his goals were not unrealistic.

Six months before his twenty-second birthday, there was still no concrete plan proposed by our local Regional Center, and I was told that it was too early to plan. I did my homework and found the service provider that had the same philosophy and approach to people as my family's.

The ongoing "negotiations" with the Regional Center to provide the support person Jeremy needs for part of each weekday to continue working on his goals of learning at college while using his skills to earn money created much stress for our family. Although I had organized a backup plan so that nothing would change in Jeremy's day-to-day schedule, Jeremy became very agitated and developed symptoms of post-traumatic stress disorder. He could not leave the house, and I could not leave him alone with support staff. He missed the start of the new semester, eventually becoming able to attend after receiving treatment from a trauma therapist. Meanwhile, I developed some health issues, and I realized that for us to stay healthy, we needed to develop a game plan that would work for our family. Jeremy's goals to be fully included in society and to earn a living rested on principles that were ethical and sound, and I was not willing to let the systems in place and their budgeting issues in this economy dictate Jeremy's quality of life. There is freedom from stress in deciding that come what may, you will stick to your principles and find a way to reach your goals.

JEREMY:

Unlike for neurotypical people, when transition occurs for people with autism like me, the process is very difficult. When I left the high school at age twenty-two, my mom and I had a plan. My mom had organized this plan for a long time, but the Regional Center did not back up what they had been agreeing to in theory. They did not have another acceptable plan ready despite my mom and school team working with them for a long time. My mom was planning ahead, but the systems in the great state of California were not cooperating. Being very nervous, I felt like I needed lots of medication, but I knew medication was not a good solution. I was very upset because I felt my mom was doing everything.

Basically the people in power refused to give an answer to our request for a long time. They said they needed to plan for all young adults with autism leaving school before replying, even though we were supposed to have an Individual Program Plan for me. This created a lot of stress for me and my family.

The disturbing thing is, if I and other people with developmental disabilities did not exist, the people in power would have no job. People make money because we exist, but they have a hard time responding to our needs, citing the lack of money. The systems in place are not cost-effective if they have money for salaries for the persons in power, but not enough money for the supports that people need to live and be productive. I think the systems are like big machines and you get what you need only if you stand up like David did to Goliath. David won in the end. The lesson is be brave and stick to your principles.

THE PARENTS

Parents and educators often commiserate about how challenging transitions are for our loved ones on the autism spectrum. Rarely do we acknowledge that they are difficult for us as well.

The transition into adulthood is probably the hardest. For the young adult, there is the loss of structure that school provided for six hours a day as well as the loss of contact with people he saw every day for years. For the parent there is the loss of regular access to and support from educators and therapists. For those whose children require continual supervision, there is the loss of six hours a day when a parent had coverage for their child.

As parents, we are facing transitions in other areas of our lives. Some of us have to care for our elderly parents. For those whose children are still living at home and require 24/7 supports, it can feel like we spend our life sandwiched between our parents and our children. Some of us are going through our own midlife crisis. Yet even though we need some space to figure things out about ourselves, we find our children need us more than ever.

It is important to note that the stress we feel as parents is not generated by our adult child with autism, but rather from the failings of the systems in place that are supposedly there to help us. There are caring people in the system, yet often the lack of options and foresight and inability to plan ahead or provide options for our loved ones are accepted as normal by the systems in place. This is what created the most stress in our family.

You Are Not Alone

The parent-child relationship is one of the most enduring social ties that human beings have. Over time, as the neurotypical child matures, the relationship shifts and progresses, and eventually the parent stops being responsible for them and their actions. Not so for parents of children on the autism spectrum.

Research shows that mothers of children with an autism spectrum disorder (ASD) continue to worry throughout their child's life span. A particular time of stress is the transition from public education services. Mothers of teens and adults on the spectrum experience chronic stress, struggling with frequent fatigue and work interruptions. Researchers have found that a hormone associated with stress was extremely low in these women, consistent with people experiencing chronic stress, such as soldiers in combat. Ongoing stresses include managing problematic behaviors and dealing with the losses of expectations associated with having a child whose development is not neurotypical.

Having an adult child with autism creates more financial stress. Families tend to have nearly one-third less income than those with typically developing children. There is likely to be one breadwinner because mothers of children with autism are less likely to work, and when they are employed, these moms tend to earn less than others.

Many parents worry that their adult children's basic needs for employment, housing, transportation, social interactions, recreation, health care, and financial security will not be met. And rightly so. According to an Easter Seals Survey carried out in 2010:

- Nearly 7 in 10 adults with disabilities (69 percent) lived with their parents (or their guardian); only 17 percent lived independently compared to more than half of adult children without disabilities (51 percent).
- Just 11 percent of parents of children with a disability stated their child was employed full-time.
- Only 6 in 10 rated their child's quality of life as excellent or good (61 percent), compared to 8 in 10 parents of adults without a disability (82 percent).
- Parents assessed their child's ability to manage their own finances at 34 percent, compared to 82 percent of parents of adults without disabilities.
- Parents rated their child's having the life skills necessary to live independently at 30 percent, versus 83 percent of parents of adults without disabilities.

All this is to say that our fears are well grounded, and we have company.

There are some positives associated with having our grown children still living with us. Studies show that mothers are agents of positive change in their child's life. The family helps the adult child develop and improve his behavior while the family also benefits from and enjoys the company of the adult child. The effect of having a sibling with autism has a wide range of impacts, both positive and negative, that continue into adulthood.

THE YOUNG ADULT

Many parents are apprehensive about the teen and adult years, and they fear that their adult child may "get worse" as they get older. However, the reality is that maladaptive behaviors, such as temper tantrums and self-injury associated with autism, generally subside with age. Research shows some improvement for many in verbal communication, and social reciprocity such as social smiling and eye gazing tend to improve. Other improvements include social and daily living skills, repetitive behaviors, and emotional responsiveness, such as offering comfort to a distressed parent. There is hope as well that the current young teens who have benefited from earlier intervention than the current adults with autism will show even more improvements.

However, research also reports that there is a high risk of depression in young adults with Asperger's Syndrome. In a Swedish study published in September 2011, 70 percent had experienced at least one episode of major depression, half of them had experienced recurring depression, and 56 percent met criteria for at least one anxiety disorder.

If the transition out of high school into adulthood is difficult for the parent, imagine how difficult it is for the young adult. For years he has been going to school for six hours a day and has had a regular schedule, and now his whole world changes. Even if your adult child can communicate, he is probably not good at communicating how he is feeling. Some may communicate the only way they know how: through behaviors that are inappropriate and make life difficult at home.

If your child is on the more able end of the spectrum and attends college, he may have difficulties with the lack of structure and with planning the use of his time to keep up with the workload. The person leaving the school transition program may have a volunteer position or a job ten hours a week but may have difficulty with the unstructured times.

It is important that as a parent you prepare your adult child for the transition. For those on the less able end of the spectrum, it is important to take the time to explain what is happening and what will happen. If social stories with pictures have been useful before, use them now as well. Even if they are unable to communicate with you very well, they probably understand a good portion of what you are saying.

Treating Them as Adults

This transition period is also a time to reflect upon how we view and treat our adult child. As parents, we need to acknowledge and accept that we will be parenting our loved ones on the spectrum a lot longer than our neurotypical children. We have to walk a fine line between being supportive and overly protective of our adult children. Our adult child is just that—an adult—and we need to acknowledge that and all that it entails. With neurotypical offspring, we remember to give them more freedom because they argue for it—as they get older, they express their desire for more independence. As your youth on the spectrum gets older, you will need to find ways to make them more independent of you. In many cases with an adult child who needs supports, the parent will have to do the pulling away. It is important to do this, but it is difficult as well. It depends on the particular circumstances when the parent should begin this process. But adult children need to experience other people and relationships.

One major concern for our children is safety, no matter where they are on the spectrum. We need to teach our children safety skills as much as possible. We can make decisions thinking of our adult children's safety, but we can't protect them too much or they will not experience activities or situations that will help them grow. What we need to do over time is teach them how to make wise decisions and surround them with the right kind of people who will help them or advise them in their decision making, and some ideas will be discussed in Chapter 2.

Although for some the idea of having their dependent adult child live away from them is frightening, research shows that mothers whose adult children lived apart from them reported that the greatest positive impact of the move was on the child himself, as there was more opportunity for independence and continuing development.

QUALITY OF LIFE

Most parents would agree that the thing they most wish for their adult child—on or off the spectrum—is a good quality of life. This is defined as the degree to which an individual can enjoy the important possibilities of his or her life, based on the opportunities and limitations each person has. Quality of life also reflects the interaction of personal and environmental factors. In many respects, our psychological attitude defines our satisfaction with our life.

But what about those with autism who have little control over their lives and need supports, or those with Asperger's who may be independent but don't have a social network? According to a ten-year research study by the Quality of Life Research Unit at the University of Toronto, the quality of life of people with developmental disabilities is directly related to the degree to which they have the opportunities to make decisions, especially for those who are nonverbal. They also suggested that the quality of life of those with a developmental disability who live more independently would be enhanced by receiving more practical and emotional support.

Luckily, there are tools that can help you and your adult child together plan a life based on his interests and his strengths, and create lifelong personal and community supports. In Chapter 2 we will discuss these processes.

Self-Determination

If quality of life is the opportunity to make decisions, then giving people the right to make decisions is the guiding principle behind self-determination. In the mid-1990s, self-determination was implemented in some states in the hopes of providing a more cost-effective system for serving those with developmental disabilities while at the same time giving those persons and their families more choice in determining the services they receive. Studies carried out over ten years indicate that individuals enjoyed an increased quality of life while saving the states money. The self-determination movement gave state officials a new set of tools to increase the efficiency of present systems and meet the aspirations of people with disabilities. However, it is unclear how the new economy, coupled with the rise of adults with autism entering the system, is affecting the initiatives that were begun.

JEREMY:

In the past people like me did not get a formal education. Now we feel more empowered to live a fully included life in the community. Unfortunately, adult services have not kept up with this reality. The present state budget problems make it worse, but the real problem lies with the system's attitude.

As an adult with a developmental disability, I have the right under the Lanterman Act to live in my community as any neuro-typical person does. The Lanterman Act was passed in California in 1977 and gives people with developmental disabilities the right to supports needed to live as independent a life as possible. The California Regional Centers are mandated to ensure that we get the supports we need to live in our communities. However, when the

Lanterman Act was voted in, adult services were probably not expecting people like me to be able to learn and get an education. It was easier then when they left the K–12 school districts to place them in sheltered workshops (segregated employment environments where disabled people earn less than minimum wage). Now educational provisions have improved for students with disabilities, and many have been able to graduate.

My mom explained that in San Diego it is easier to get supports if the individuals do not live at home with their parents. The thing is, the Lanterman Act exists in California to help people with developmental disabilities be able to stay in their home communities and with their family. However, I might have to live away from my family to get the supports I need.

I believe that the rights of all disabled persons are covered by various laws, but most importantly they are also founded on the Fourteenth Amendment of the Constitution. The authors of that document believed that all men were created equal and that every person had the right to the pursuit of happiness. What makes me happy is learning and being able to earn a living. This is not an unrealistic goal.

THE TRANSITION PARENT'S SURVIVAL GUIDE: FROM HOPING AND COPING TO THRIVING AND SURVIVING

The last few years have been full of important life transitions in our family. My father became very ill with lung cancer and passed away. My husband, Daniel, lost his job in San Diego, and had to move to LA for a new one the same week my daughter, Rebecca, moved away to college. Jeremy and I "lost" two family members, and it was quite an adjustment. I was left living alone with Jeremy, who requires twenty-four-hour supports.

Meanwhile, Jeremy's transition to adult services did not go smoothly, despite our every attempt to work with the system. Our experience is not unusual. A proactive optimist at heart, I was not prepared for how laborious, discouraging, and depressing the process would be. After much soul-searching I decided that if we were going not only to survive, but actually to enjoy a good quality of life in this new phase of our lives, we needed to make some changes about how we were planning for the future. We started by defining what was important to us based on our principles, exploring our options, envisioning and creating new ones, and then developing a game plan that worked for us. Transition is a process, and with the right perspective it can be enriching and rewarding.

In the following chapters you will find information and tips for each particular area important to adult life such as relationships, employment, housing, and so on. Here are some recommended steps to help you stay focused on what is important to you and your family, while you are creating a future based on your beliefs:

1. **Clarify your family's principles surrounding the notion of disability.** This step is important, as it drives the rest. What principles does your family believe to be the most important? Do you believe in self-determination, in the right of your adult child to make decisions or have input in the decision-making process? Do you believe in full inclusion or segregation, or something in between?

2. **Establish short-term and long-term goals.** Start by discussing both with your adult child. If your adult child does not communicate effectively, then figure out what his strengths, choices, and joys are with the help of people who know him well. There are some great tools, such as PATH, which are extremely helpful for facilitating these discussions, and they are described in Chapter 2. Make sure your goals are clear and concise.

3. **Let your principles and goals drive your decisions and your actions.** As you will see throughout the book, sometimes the systems in place are unable to support your goals. Revisit your principles (i.e., full inclusion in

the community) and the options the systems have to offer. If the options are based on the same principles, you may be able to work with the system to create a solution. If not, and if your principles are important to you, then find a way to create a solution without the systems. Some solutions you may be able to create on your own (i.e., self-employment options). For other solutions (such as housing) you may need to find other like-minded parents and professionals to work with to create acceptable options. (You will find examples in the following chapters.)

4. **Realize which things you have control over and which you do not.** You have control over your family's individual and collective goals based on your principles, but you have no direct control over the economy or the funding guidelines put into place by the systems in power. You have control over the things you own and how you spend your money. You have direct control over your actions and your emotions. In other words, you cannot always control what happens to you, but you can control how you decide to react.

5. **Plan how you are going to reach your goals.** If your plan relies on systems or funding over which you have no control, then have a Plan B, and even a Plan C, ready so that if you cannot find or create a workable solution with the systems in place, you still have an acceptable plan. There is freedom in knowing that you have options, and that you do not have to accept options that are not in line with your principles.

6. **Find like-minded people who have the same goals.** It is clear that there are not enough options for all adults on the spectrum. Other people have done what you have, or are looking into doing so. Why reinvent the wheel? Together you have more power and can share resources, or at least have like-minded people with

whom to brainstorm. When enough like-minded people get together, systems can change.

7. **Take care of yourself.** There is only one you. Make sure you are taking good care of your health, eating and exercising, and taking breaks. Don't lose "yourself" in the process of transitioning your adult child. Make room for whatever gives you joy in your life. If you are unhealthy or unhappy, you won't be enjoying the process, and neither will your adult child. You deserve to have some time to yourself to do what you enjoy doing, so carve out some time for yourself and make it happen. Even if it is only twenty minutes a day or a few hours a week, take time out for yourself. Don't lose sight of YOU.

Focusing on what is important to your adult child and the family is empowering. By knowing what your goals are, you will be better prepared to analyze your family's needs, the existing options, and the creation of new ones. Remember that it is a process, and do not get discouraged. Creating an adult life for anyone is quite a journey!

JEREMY'S TOP TEN TIPS TO PARENTS ON THE TRANSITION TO ADULT LIFE

1. **Believe in yourself.** If you know what your adult child wants, you will do the right thing. Do not doubt that you are the expert on your son or daughter. You have done your best so far, and you can be their guiding light for the future.

2. **Inspire your adult child to have his own life.** Like it or not, your child is an adult. Treat him in an appropriate manner. Sometimes you will need to guide your adult child in decision making.

3. **Help them have access to adult mentors.** Teach them how to ask questions from trusted adults. Give them the

opportunity to listen to the opinion of others so they can carefully analyze their situation by hearing what the mentors have to say. They need to have a coach other than the parent.

4. **Help your adult child behave appropriately.** They are expected to behave as an adult. Tell them you, as a parent, may seem stressed, but it is not because of them; it is because of the system. If they don't know why you are stressed, they will get nervous and overwhelmed and be unable to control their emotions and actions. Look for the nice things they can do. Give them the opportunity to do something fun.

5. **Tell your adult child that change will be happening.** Explain the reason for the change so that they can prepare for transition. Get them to believe that they will be ready for a new, meaningful life. This helps your adult child have behaviors that are appropriate.

6. **Tell your adult child to be patient.** It will take time for you to figure things out, so he will need to be waiting. The best thing is for him to know from the beginning that you will be working on it for some time.

7. **Set clear goals.** Nothing is worse than having doubts that the system is really on the same path as you are despite years of apparent agreement. Realize that your hope is not in the hands of others. You must create your own future.

8. **Have the idea to be independent of the system.** Basically do this until the day they realize that the right thing to do is to allow your adult child to live a decent life just like any other human. It is not a choice to give up on your child.

9. **Assure your adult child you are doing your best.** They need to hear you say this, and to say that you will not give up. Your adult child needs to hear the realities but also what you are doing about it.

10. **Become political.** Let your lawmakers know that life is hard because the systems are not working. Eventually the systems will have to change. But they will not change unless we make them realize we will not accept being just another line item on a budget.

RESOURCES

Books

Adolescents on the Autism Spectrum: A Parent's Guide to the Cognitive, Social, Physical, and Transition Needs of Teenagers with Autism Spectrum Disorders (Penguin), Chantal Sicile-Kira
Articles on author website, www.ChantalSicile-Kira.com
Autism Speaks Family Services Transition Tool Kit, http://www .autismspeaks.org/family-services/tool-kits/transition-tool-kit
Life Journey Through Autism: A Guide for Transition to Adulthood, http://www.researchautism.org/resources/guidebook.asp
Movement Differences and Diversity in Autism/Mental Retardation: Appreciating and Accommodating People with Communication and Behavior Challenges (DRI Press), Anne M. Donnellan and Martha R. Leary

Websites

AUTCOM—The Autism National Committee, http://www .autcom.org/
Autism College.com, http://autismcollege.com/
Autism One, http://www.autismone.org/
Autism Research Institute, http://www.autism.com/
Autism Society of America, http://www.autism-society.org/
Autism Speaks, http://www.autismspeaks.org/
Autistic Global Initiative, http://www.autismwebsite.com/agi/index .html
The Autistic Self Advocacy Network, http://www.autisticadvocacy .org/

GRASP—The Global Regional Asperger Syndrome Partnership, http://www.grasp.org/

National Autism Association, http://www.nationalautismassociation .org/

The National Autism Resource and Information Center, http:// autismnow.org/about-us/

TASH, http://tash.org/

CHAPTER 2

CREATING LIFELONG COMMUNITY AND PERSONAL SUPPORTS

My mom is my greatest advocate, but she wants me to have other people to help me make decisions. I need an advisory board that I can call upon to advise me on matters of importance.

—Jeremy

As Jeremy has gotten older, my concerns about him have increased. As he grew up, the only certainty we had was that we wanted him to live fully included in the community of his choosing. Our concern then shifted to who would help him make decisions and advocate on his behalf when we were gone. Jeremy has one sister, Rebecca, three years his junior, but we do not want all the responsibilities to rest on her shoulders.

Jeremy has always enjoyed city and suburban life and has not shown an interest in living in rural areas. For him to be included in his community we have to develop natural supports, and Jeremy has to find ways to give back to his community. It's a process, and it doesn't happen overnight. But I feel confident that we are on the right track to creating the supports Jeremy needs that are not dependent solely on us.

JEREMY:

My behavior is such that I can live at home, but my mom is tired and I need younger people to go out with in the evenings. I also need a circle of support to learn about life, and to learn about how the rest of the world communicates to have social interaction. I need to be around neurotypical people in order to have opportunities to talk about things that people our age know from experience. For example, I enjoy happy hour, but I don't know where to go and need friends to go with. New friends and new places are hard to find when you need a piece of technology to communicate. Friends are a necessary part of everyone's circle of support.

THE NEED FOR COMMUNITY SUPPORTS

Neurotypical children need less and less of their parents' help the older they get. This is not the case with many children on the spectrum. There are adults with Asperger's who are completely independent; however, there are many who still need mentoring or more supports. For most of us with children requiring twenty-four-hour supports, there are concerns about who is going to care for our adult child. For all of us parents, it's the big, scary question, "What is going to happen to them after we are gone?"

If your adult child with autism has siblings, hopefully they will be able to be there as a support in many ways. If they have only one sibling, extra supports may be needed so that sibling does not feel overwhelmed. Ways of creating these structures of support are discussed in this chapter.

Besides having concerns about who will care for them and who will pay the bills, we have concerns about how our loved one will spend his time, and about where and whom he will spend it with. Relationships with people who care about him who are not paid to do so are not made overnight.

Some adults with autism live at home for a long time, and when the parents pass away, so does the community support. Some may live in secluded communities that may have natural community supports built into the way of life. Still others live in group homes in cities or suburban areas where community supports may be based on the people you live with and the people who work at the group home. Others may live in supported living, and unless they are interdependent and good at creating connections with others, they may find their community connections limited and dependent on their roommate.

Although some caretakers and support staff may over time become lifelong supports, it's never a good idea to have a person's community and support connections dependent on only paid staff or a paid agency, or dependent on one organization or service provider.

JEREMY:

The Importance of Family Supports

I like to find my old stim toys because they're like old friends. Certain toys bring back memories. A Christmas stocking that I like reminds me of celebrating the holidays. I remember that Mom had a dinner for the family: Grandma and Grandpa, Aunt Monica, and Aunt Christine. I got the meaning of what family life is truly about. The aunts were so happy to be there, and Mom told them that doing this every year was a tradition. Mom explained to Rebecca that family was family, and Mom expected we would do this when Mom and Dad got older. The Christmas stocking truly symbolizes the idea of family for me.

HOW TO CREATE COMMUNITY SUPPORTS

Oftentimes parents comment on the lack of friends or natural supports that exist in the life of their teen or young adult on the spectrum. If a person has difficulties initiating and establishing social relationships and communicating with others, it is likely that their circles of supports are small and that they need expanding. Parents may need to help facilitate and nurture supports, based on their adult child's needs and desires.

Circle of Supports

Most of us have naturally been creating different circles of supports since birth. We've been creating networks of people who connect with us on different levels—some whom we are very close to, others we are just acquainted with, some who are work colleagues we like but may not be particularly close to. Judith Snow, M.A., is a social innovator, a visual artist, and an advocate for inclusion who became the first person in Canada to receive government-mandated individualized funding for personal assistance. She describes the different circles of supports as follows:

- **Circle of Intimacy.** Includes those with whom we share our secrets, have great intimacy and emotions. These are people, animals, and for some, objects that are so important to us that their absence would affect us in a major way. Family members are usually included here, but not always.
- **Circle of Friendship.** Includes those who are friends or relatives whom we see occasionally for dinner or a movie, but who are not our closest friends we need to see on a regular basis.
- **Circle of Participation.** Includes the organizations or people you participate with in your life such as your job,

your place of worship, schools, organizations—places where you participate and interact with people. This circle contains people who may eventually be in the Circle of Friendship or even of Intimacy.
- **Circle of Exchange.** Includes the people who are paid to be in our lives such as therapists, doctors, teachers, haircutters, and so on.

Almost all neurotypicals or nondisabled people have a fair number of people in all four circles. However, those with disabilities—including autism—have practically all the people they know clustered into the Circle of Intimacy (i.e., family) and the Circle of Exchange (paid service providers). Having connections only on these two levels helps create the emotional and financial strain on the family that most of us parents of loved ones on the spectrum feel. What is needed is more connections to organizations and areas of interest (Circle of Participation) where there is the possibility of meeting people who eventually become friends (Circle of Friendship). This not only will provide more quality of life for your adult child, but will remove some of the strain on the family. The young adult and his parents need to create a circle of support of people who care about their adult child but who are not related to them, and who are not currently paid to care for them. These may be former tutors, therapists, or teachers, people from church or school with whom they have developed relationships.

It does take planning to create the Circle of Participation and the Circle of Friendship. For someone like Jeremy who needs a support person and uses assistive technology to communicate but does not easily initiate, it's not been easy. However, it is easier now than when he was a teenager. For Jeremy we looked at his interests—writing, autism, and advocacy—and focused on finding how he could meet people or get involved in organizations.

JEREMY:

My Mentors: "Team Jeremy"

My life has not been easy. The reality is that being stuck in a body that doesn't always do what I want it to makes everyday life hard. Frankly I do not believe that my life would be worth living if it were not for the team of people that my mom has found and coached over the years. Just like a sports team, all the members of the team rely on each team member doing its best, including me.

Recently I had to take a test that was proctored. I take my tests separately from the other students, in a quiet room with a proctor and my support person. I use a wireless keyboard and iPad, which has a voice-output application, to give answers. The support person assists with setting up the equipment and reading the test questions to me. I am supposed to wear prism glasses that help with vision processing, but I have a hard time wearing glasses on my nose because my face is very sensitive.

I knew the material, but I was extremely nervous because I had a new support person. I should have tried to explain to the support person and the proctor why I was uncomfortable, but I got stuck in my body, so I had trouble controlling my motor movements to point accurately to the letters on my keyboard, and so I failed the test.

The Team Jeremy coach (Mom) said, "It's okay, but now you know why I want you to practice and to wear your glasses for typing. It's your choice. But remember, the more you practice the more your muscles develop motor memory and better movement initiation. You know your eye-hand coordination and eye convergence gets better with practice, too." If I don't practice, I am letting Team Jeremy down, because when you are part of a team, you must do your best.

The evening of the day I failed the test, I was scheduled to speak to twenty-two members of a college softball team. I talked about how team members have to be able to count on each other. I told them (with the help of my iPad and the voice-output app), "Needing a team of people in order to reach my goals is a fact of life for me. I am dependent on others for most of my needs to be met. Being a part of my team means that a person agrees to work with the others to help me reach my goals. This takes practice to be the best we can while watching out for the others so we can do the best possible. I know you lost your games today, but did you play your best, and did you watch out for each other? That is what a team player does."

Then I talked about having to overcome the obstacle of having autism. The softball coach asked how I got over some major challenges to get where I am today. I told her that when you hit a wall, you must pick yourself up and keep on going. When you are physically dependent on others, it is really hard. You know that overcoming challenges is necessary for your sanity. Luckily I have Team Jeremy to help me reach my goals.

CREATING CONNECTIONS

Volunteering in the community is a good way of creating connections (Circle of Participation). It's also a way for your son or daughter to discover what they are good at or what they like, to learn responsibility, and to give back to the community. They learn the enjoyment of giving and not just receiving.

When Jeremy was thirteen or fourteen, we decided that it was time to try some kind of volunteering. At that time, Jeremy did not have a lot of appropriate communication skills, but he liked being out and about and had appropriate behavior. We picked Meals on Wheels because he liked riding in the car, and he could ring the doorbell and hand people their meals. Many of the people on our route were elderly and in apartments, and they were so happy to see a young person at the door. The hardest parts of this volunteer experience were that often the elderly residents had decorations on their front doors that Jeremy had a hard time keeping his hands off, and that when the door was open he wanted to go inside to check out the place.

Next he started walking the dogs for a pet shop near where one of his support persons lived. This position served the dual purpose of helping out a harried shopkeeper and teaching Jeremy how to hold a leash and walk a dog, good practice for owning your own pet. When Jeremy got his assistance dog,

Handsome, we started taking him to visit relatives and friends in hospitals or nursing homes. The staff and other patients love spending time with Handsome, and Jeremy enjoys seeing how happy Handsome makes the people.

Meanwhile, as Jeremy's written communication skills improved over the years and he started writing articles about what it's like to have autism and how that affected him, he began to receive emails and messages through Facebook from parents saying how much they appreciated his insight, how helpful it was to them to have his point of view on his experience. He would answer their questions, and over time he realized that he had plenty of insight to offer to others and decided that he wanted to become a writer and an advocate to help others. He hopes to give back to the community in this way.

More recently, Jeremy joined the staff of his community college newspaper and a local nonprofit writers' association. He is also attending and participating in autism conferences. There are many opportunities available to become involved, and hopefully this will broaden his circle of supports over time.

PERSON CENTERED PLANNING: WHAT IS IMPORTANT TO YOUR ADULT CHILD?

Person Centered Planning (PCP) is a problem-solving process whose focus is to help a person with a developmental disability plan the life that he or she wants. In PCP, a group of people who care about the person get together and share information and figure out how to support the person in planning his life. For those who are unable to communicate effectively, it is even more important to have people involved who know the person well enough in different areas of the person's life in order to help give input about what appears to be important to that person. A great resource in developing Person Centered Planning is Inclusion Press's *All My Life's a Circle: Using the Tools: Circles,*

Maps & Paths, by Falvey, Forest, Pierpoint, and Rosenberg, who developed the processes described below.

Some of the tools used in Person Centered Planning include the following:

- **MAPS** is a graphic planning tool that starts with the history of the person that each individual present shares to create a picture of what the person is like; then the individual shares his dreams as well as his fears, and what direction he wants to move in.
- **Essential Lifestyle Planning** is a process for figuring out how a person wants to live and then developing a plan to make it happen. Items discussed include what is important to the person in everyday life and what others need to know and do to address issues of safety and health while still keeping present what is important in that person's life.
- **PATH** is a creative process that works backward, starting with the person's wishes for the future and moving toward what first steps can be taken now to go in that direction, identifying who can help the person reach his goals.

Even for those with limited communication skills, all of the above can be accomplished by having people important to that person present. They can help draw a picture of the person and their imagined future based on what they know that he enjoys, in order to ensure a good quality of life. Those who are on the more able end of the spectrum may find these tools useful as a way to help with goal setting and clarifying their own personal vision. Many neurotypical people have used the PATH to ensure that everything they do is in line with their future goals.

Parents using planning tools such as MAPS and PATH report feeling more supported while planning for their child's future. Beth and Steve are parents to seventeen-year-old Kevin, who has limited speech, and live in New Jersey. They have concerns about the future and were not comfortable with some of the options that they were being presented with as possibilities for his adult life, such as sheltered workshop (restrictive environments where workers are paid substandard wages). Beth and Steve organized a MAPS planning session with an experienced facilitator in which they explored Kevin's strengths, likes, and opportunities with others who knew him well. After the session, Beth and Steve felt heartened and encouraged by a team of people who now had a shared perspective of what the future could hold for their son. Although Beth and Steve are the ones who will have to make it happen, they know they have a community of people willing to help them any way they can.

JEREMY:

For the PATH I imagined my future without barriers. I have the freedom to decide my future, but doing a PATH can be fearful. Facets of life are hard to dare to dream about. It feels a lot like what fame does to people aspiring to act: they hope to be famous, but when they are, they can't handle the pressure. In a PATH, people encourage you to be bold and take responsibility for your dreams. When you trust in your ability to dream, you have greater results during the PATH process. The life I want to have is happy and full of people who can help me. My future life includes my own house, a beautiful wife, my freedom to dream, writing to earn money, and advocacy. Having a PATH can help me accomplish the goals I want. I am fearful, but I know it is because I am so young. Facing my fears is a challenge, but with help I will succeed.

Jeremy participated in a MAPS planning process when he was in junior high. Then, when a service provider began providing supports, they organized an Essential Lifestyle Planning for Jeremy. They asked Jeremy to invite the people who were most important to him to come together. The purpose was for the agency to get to know Jeremy and to make the transition as seamless as possible. Those who could not be there joined by Skype or gave their input by answering questions in an email. Some of the questions discussed were:

- Gifts: What does Jeremy contribute to his surroundings; what do others appreciate about him?
- Circle of Support: Who are the people Jeremy counts on?
- Who is Jeremy: What is unique about him? How would you describe him in one word?
- Health ⏐ Safety: What do we need to know in order to keep Jeremy healthy and safe?
- Non-negotiables: What must Jeremy "have, do, and be"? What can he not imagine living without?
- What do we need to know about Jeremy in order to be successful in supporting him?
- Communication Log: If Jeremy does this _____, we think it means _____, and we should _____.
- Triggers: What are the things that can cause a "reaction," either good or bad?
- Action Plan: What do we do now?

This gathering was very important as the agency got to know Jeremy, and Jeremy became aware that they were interested in him as a person. As you can tell by the questions, the kind of information gathered was a great way for the agency to find out how to best support Jeremy. (More about service provider agencies can be found in Chapter 7.) This kind of information gathering works even for a person who does not have great communication skills.

Then, as Jeremy started talking more and more about his future goals, we were offered the opportunity to participate in a PATH planning process. Again, Jeremy invited the people important to him to attend. The gathering started with Jeremy describing what, if there were no obstacles, he wanted his life to look like in five years. Meanwhile, someone drew representations and words following Jeremy's directives on a large banner of paper taped to the wall. Then he described what his life would look like a year from now, and Jeremy named which people could help him in the different areas of his life to make his dreams a reality. Finally, Jeremy decided on some steps to move forward. The people present identified how they could help him reach his goals, and Jeremy thought of a few other people to ask to help him. In this process, Jeremy was practicing interdependence (i.e., asking people for help in areas they had skills), self-advocacy, self-determination, and responsibility.

This process is very goal oriented and efficient. It keeps people focused on the goal and keeps us going forward. For those like Jeremy who are dependent on others and the systems in place, a PATH planning process can help keep the focus on what the person's important life goals are. In this way, you will be clear on what your adult child's goals are, and this will clarify what you need to do. Remember, your loved one's quality of life depends on your working on his goals for the life he wants. Often, the systems in place are trying to fit your adult child into their preconceived ideas of what your adult child's life should look like. By being clear on your child's goals and needs, you can stay focused and work with the system, or find creative ways to create your child's future life, perhaps with other like-minded parents, professionals, and nonprofit organizations in your community.

PLANNING AHEAD: LEGAL AND FINANCIAL CONCERNS

Laws may vary from state to state when it comes to legal and financial issues, so make sure you get the correct information for your state. Check with your local autism or disability organizations in your area, as well as your state's Developmental Disabilities Services website. Here are some tips:

- If you have not done so already, look into conservatorship or adult guardianship of your child when he turns eighteen, if it is appropriate in your child's situation. Laws may vary in each state.
- Decide who will be your child's guardian or conservator in the event of your death. Make sure to develop your will and an estate plan, including a special needs trust.
- The estate plan including a special needs trust will maximize your loved one's wealth after you die. Even if you have nothing right now, you want to make sure the structures are in place so that if you have life insurance, or if a relative leaves your child money, it goes into a trust fund.
- Ensure that there is financial planning in conjunction with legal planning that will safeguard Social Security and Medicare benefits (federal health insurance for certain people with disabilities), as well as any possible inheritance.
- Have guidelines for establishing or maintaining state and federal benefits.
- Do some financial planning to ensure that the extras in life, such as cable TV, vacations, favorite books and entertainment, and favorite clothing styles that may have been provided by the family, can continue to be provided.
- Try to predict likely medical needs and desired interventions and their costs so they can be taken into consideration when planning.
- Incorporate the cost of residential needs depending on your adult child's living arrangements.
- Make sure that your and your adult child's vision of what his future should look like is clarified and documented.
- If your adult child is not independent, create a video showing your adult child in his daily activities and the kind of assistance he needs, as well as illustrating his likes and strengths.

- Ensure that detailed choices your adult child may wish to make beyond basic food, housing, and medical needs are documented.
- Review these every three to five years.

CREATING STRUCTURES TO PROVIDE PERSONALIZED SUPPORTS AND SERVICES

One way of providing a structure to oversee financial, legal, and quality-of-life supports is through the creation of a Microboard, a small, nonprofit corporation with the specific intent of supporting an individual with a disability. Not only are these structures, if done properly, a good way to plan for the future, but they're also a way to carefully establish community and personal supports over time. The result is a board of trusted advisors that will be there when your loved one needs assistance in making decisions, or needs decisions made for him. They also provide oversight and peace of mind in ensuring things are done correctly. Microboards are designed to serve the person with the disability. There is a Board of Directors made up of friends and family members who have voting powers. The board members do not receive money for services from your child in any way (i.e., service providers). In this way, control of the essential resources stays in the hands of the person on the spectrum and his or her closest and trusted allies.

Parents who have put Microboards in place for their children praise their many benefits. A Microboard can help raise money for needed purchases and expenses and training not covered by insurance or other sources. A Microboard helps develop friends and expand the circle of supports. Parents report that planning meetings takes some effort and organization, but the results are strengthening and empowering for the person who is the focus as well as for all involved. For more information on Microboards, go to http://www.communityworks.info/articles/microboard.htm. Microboards currently exist in some states. If they do not exist in your state yet, it does not mean you can't set one up, although you have to be careful to do things in accordance with your state laws. Contact Microboard associations in other states for details.

Another option is to create a Human Service Cooperative with other like-minded parents and young adults. Human Service Cooperatives play a role that is similar to traditional service-provider agencies (discussed in Chapter 7), with one major difference: member-owners are the individual people who are served and their personal representatives (usually close friends and family members). They are the governing authority, and the responsibility is placed entirely in their hands. This kind of empowerment gives people control of their human services, including power over their choices and control of their lives.

JEREMY:

I get nervous thinking about when my parents will die. My other relatives live far away and they have their own lives. I hope that my sister will be there for me. Creating a formal support network is a great idea, but it takes work, and who will do this when my parents are gone? Frankly, I need people I trust to help me find the resources I need. Having an advisory board made up of close friends and relatives is my goal.

JEREMY'S TOP TEN TIPS FOR CREATING LIFELONG COMMUNITY SUPPORTS

1. **Make connections.** You can help your child by helping him find people who share his interests. There are many different hobby clubs and associations. Look for the kind of activities where your child can grow deeper relationships with the participants. Help him grow in this way.

2. **Help your child adjust to life changes.** When a sibling moves out, suggest setting up a schedule of visits in person or by Skype. Tell him it is hard to handle the change, but it will get better.

3. **Teach your child appropriate behaviors.** Explain to your child that it's easier to make friends when his behavior isn't threatening. Try to teach him to control his need to move all around the place, because neurotypicals are nervous when he does that.

4. **Teach your adult child how to volunteer.** She will learn to give back to the community and make some connections who might become friends.

5. **Love your adult child for what he is and not for what he could become.** We very much want to become better people, but we really need to be accepted for what we are without being expected to be neurotypical.

6. **Not all people are understanding of others.** Be aware that there are no guarantees that all people are willing to be with people who are different.

7. **Pick your Microboard wisely.** Identify people who have your child's best interest at heart. Recognize people who are willing to love your child for who he is even if he doesn't seem like the kind with whom you would socialize.

8. **Stay healthy and take breaks.** Your child cares about you, and you must take care of yourself first before you can help your child.

9. **Believe in your child.** Help him discover his strengths, because often people focus on his deficits.

10. **Do not be afraid of the future.** Face your fears and prepare for the future you and your adult child envision. Having the support your child needs can help him become the person he wants to be. Freedom can be great but difficult for your child because it means taking responsibility for the choices involving his life.

RESOURCES

Books

A Good Life: For You and Your Relative with a Disability, Al
Etmanski, Planned Lifetime Advocacy Network, http://www
.plan.ca/

All My Life's a Circle: Using the Tools: Circles, Maps & Paths,
(Inclusion Press), Falvey, Forest, Pierpoint, and Rosenberg

*The Special Needs Planning Guide: How to Prepare for Every Stage
of Your Child's Life,* John W. Nadworny, CFP®, ChFC, and
Cynthia R. Haddad, CFP®

What's Really Worth Doing and How to Do It, Judith Snow

Websites

Community Works, http://www.communityworks.info/

Enabling Person-Directed Planning for Augmentative and
Alternative Communication (AAC) Users, http://connectability
.ca/2011/06/12/enabling-person-directed-planning-for
-augmentative-and-alternative-communication-aac-users/

Illinois Association of Microboards and Cooperatives, http://www
.iambc.org/

Inclusion Network, http://www.inclusion.com/inclusionnetwork
.html

IOD Bookstore at the University of New Hampshire Institute on
Disability, http://www.iodbookstore.com/

Microboards, http://www.communityworks.info/articles
/microboard.htm

Tennessee Association of Microboards and Cooperatives, Inc.,
http://www.tnmicroboards.org/modules.php?name=Content
&pa=showpage&pid=7

CHAPTER 3

LIFE SKILLS FOR A LIFE SPAN

I think people do not understand the challenge of getting your body and your mind to work together. This is the main problem of autism for people like me.

—Jeremy

While Jeremy was little, there were two life skill areas that I felt were the most important to teach him as they would greatly impact his quality of life as an adult. These were communication and independence. Jeremy has sensory-motor challenges, including movement differences, which affect his ability to communicate and to independently complete self-help routines. Jeremy can't always control his body; his muscles don't respond to his brain's "orders" to make them move. He also has vision-processing challenges, meaning he can see but his brain may not always process what he is seeing. Jeremy is an auditory learner, meaning that he processes what he hears better than what he sees. All these challenges impede all other areas in his life. So to teach Jeremy self-help routines we have used various techniques, including breaking down tasks into small steps and hand-over-hand prompting. It can take a long time, like trying to reestablish brain–muscle connections to stroke victims who need to relearn how to use their muscles.

When it came to communication, we tried Discrete Trial Teaching (repeated quick trials of teaching using requests, prompts, responses, and rewards); Verbal Behavior (a behavioral approach to teaching communication skills); and Picture Exchange Communication (a form of augmentative and alternative communication using picture icons). He learned some from each, but he would never get past a certain point because physically he was not able to. We tried RPM (Rapid Prompting Method), and little by little over a few years he developed the skills to point to letters on a letter board and then eventually to type on a keyboard.

JEREMY:

Life has not been easy for me. At first every professional we saw told my mom I was retarded. They only wanted my mom to give up on me. They really did not appreciate my mom telling them that she knew I could learn. My mom did not listen to negative professionals. Mom would say, "I know he is not developing normally, but show me what to do and I will teach him."

My life was saved by very good people who my mom found. The first decent reply my mom got was from a professional at a hospital in France specializing in muscle problems when I was about two years old. She told my mom that yes, there was something wrong, but to try physical therapy. The encouraging physical therapist showed my mom how to help me for more than a year. My mom and babysitter worked hard to help me learn how to move my body. I had to be moved again and again through every motion. My body could not move on its own. When I thought about moving a part of my body, nothing would happen.

I remember when my mom got me Auditory Integration Training (AIT) for the first time when I was about four or five. It was a really wonderful therapy in which I had to sit still every day for half an hour, twice a day, for two weeks, to listen to music through headphones, and it opened up a world of different sounds to me. I could hear more sounds and the voices because just until then I could not make out the differences in the noisy background. Before undergoing AIT, I would hear all sounds the same; I could not pick out the voice of the person speaking to me from the sounds in the background. I believed that all sounds were noise and did not realize that some sounds had meaning. Before AIT my mom's voice sounded like the static of a badly tuned radio frequency. It was AIT that made me understand that the noise coming out of my mom's mouth was "Jeremy" and that it was my name. AIT helped my ears "tune in" to the right radio frequency so I could hear clearly.

When my mom got tutors for me, I knew I would be able to come out of my solitude. In the UK when I was five, my mom organized a home program based on applied behavior analysis. My mom hired students, and their voices were the sweetest music to my ears. I knew that like my mom they wanted to reach me across the darkness. I get depressed about the past but not about the times Mom had tutors for me.

A few years ago, I started vision therapy. Before vision therapy I could see only fragments instead of seeing objects as a whole. Faces looked like portraits painted by Picasso. Vision therapy trained my eyes to get the whole picture of everything I see. I think vision therapy helps me to get my eyes and hands working together. The goal is to coordinate my body with my vision, and my vision with my body. It takes a great effort on my part to get my body used to my new way of seeing. It's very hard for me to control the urge to take my prism glasses off, because my body isn't used to having them on my face. The glasses are a great component to my eyes and my brain because my eyes are like a door for my brain to understand and process the world around me.

Learning is still and will always be an important part of my day. Frankly, having the ability to learn is a gift and is very rewarding just for the sake of becoming knowledgeable. Because of my autism I have to learn skills to become independent and learn how to communicate. If I can learn to be independent, I can live with roommates and have my own place.

NECESSARY LIFE SKILLS

As described in my earlier book *Autism Life Skills: Ten Essential Abilities Your Child Deserves and Needs to Learn,* there are life skills that are important to teach those on the spectrum. For some adults, learning these skills is a lifelong process. When I interviewed adults of different ability levels when writing *Autism Life Skills,* they usually mentioned the same three life skills as being most important: making sense of the world (sensory processing), communication, and safety.

There are many functional daily living skills a person needs to learn in order to become independent. It is important to focus on these, especially if someone wants more autonomy. Learning never stops, and if your adult child is not independent in some areas, he can still learn. We will be discussing more skills in the chapters on housing, college, and employment. Here, we are sharing information on general life skills.

Handling Transitions

Those interviewed shared that transitions were the most difficult area of their lives—whether transitioning from one place to another, one activity to the next, or from one major life event to another.

Yet daily life is full of transitions, which is why people on the spectrum need to learn strategies to assist them during transitions. Being prepared ahead of time is the number one strategy that helps them handle daily transitions.

People with Asperger's Syndrome have told me that they don't like change because their nervous systems have to work ten times harder to adjust. That extra work can be exhausting and sometimes mentally and physically painful. For example, Brian King, LCSW, relates that from the time he wakes up until the time he goes to sleep at night, he is constantly bombarded by sensory information that his brain does not coordinate very effectively.

If your adult child has had difficulties with transitions in the past, the transition from the schedule and environment he is used to in high school to real life may be even more difficult for him. Whether he is attending college, working, attending a day program, or at home doing nothing until services are straightened out and start up for him, he may need support. Neurotypicals experience stress when there is change (whether good or bad), and we use familiar techniques or rituals to feel comfortable in a new situation. We need to help our loved ones develop strategies to handle change, which is even more stressful for them.

Ruth is a young woman with Asperger's Syndrome who works full-time and enjoys yoga classes and going out to dinner with friends. There are times she feels overwhelmed with transitions and sensory overload. Ruth has put a picture of her favorite plush character as the wallpaper on her cell phone that she can look at when needed. This picture of a familiar and favored item helps her through those difficult moments.

Sometimes our loved ones on the spectrum need our help to find a way to reduce anxiety. Here are some tips:

- If your adult child is transitioning to college or a job, his hours may not be as set as in high school, and this may create anxiety for him. Help him set up a schedule that works for him.
- If your adult child has used transition strategies in the past—social stories, visual schedules, apps on the iPhone,

or other technological assistance—use those for the transition period. The familiarity will help ease some of the stress of dealing with new environments and schedules.

- If he is in a day program or has a job coach, see if he can use this schedule while he transitions to the new environment, and then have it fade out when no longer needed. Having something familiar in a new place where there are new people can be helpful at first.

If your child is at home with no program, it is important to encourage or put into place some kind of routine that is beneficial and enjoyable.

The Difficulties of Transitions and What Helps

JEREMY:

All daily transitions are very hard because I need to prepare my body and senses for what is coming up next. It is nice to have understanding staff, but frankly I dread transitions from one place to another.

I have lots of strategies for transitions. Knowing what is happening next is important. The hope that the following activity will be pleasant is a great motivating tool to help me through transitions. Being reminded of the rules we write together is necessary. Carrying a magazine or book is necessary.

Motivation needs to be there in order for transition to work. Treats help motivate during transitions because it is nice to have a short-term goal when working toward a long-term goal. I need the idea of a favorite food to keep motivated.

Prompting from one physical position to the next is helpful for transitions from place to place. My support staff really help me just when my body is having trouble when I can't get out of their cars. Both their voices and physical prompts help me out of the car when I can't move. It is important to have trained and understanding staff.

For successful life transitions, planning and advocating to reach your goal are necessary. Like my friend Beth says, we can make dreams come true in little steps.

COMMUNICATION

Communication and social skills will be discussed more in depth in each chapter, specifically relating to the skills needed for those topic areas (i.e., communicating on the job, at college, with support staff). But in general, communication is an area that is problematic for many, no matter their ability level. Someone on the more able end of the spectrum may take all speech literally and have challenges in understanding metaphors, idioms, and the "hidden curriculum," that is, the unwritten rules of social behavior that most of us pick up by osmosis. Many who are verbal report that during stressful situations, such as getting stopped by police while driving a car, they may freeze and be unable to speak.

These communication challenges are responsible for many on the more able end of the spectrum getting fired from their jobs or flunking out of college, as you will see when reading the personal examples shared in the chapters on college, employment, and social relationships. Miscommunication occurs with supervisors or professors, and then the individual on the spectrum gets in trouble because he can't discuss and clarify the situation to a person who has no awareness of the individual's communication challenges.

For those on the more impacted end of the spectrum who have few verbal skills, finding a way for them to communicate is important. There are both low-tech (paper and pen, letter boards) and high-tech devices (Dynavox, Lightwriter, iPad, etc.) that can bridge the divide between verbal and nonverbal. Traditionally, the high-tech devices have been expensive, although Medicare (a government-provided health insurance for those with disabilities or those over 65) pays for adults who qualify. Now it is possible to use apps on cell phones and iPads and to communicate with visual pictures or with words, or to type, and these methods are much cheaper. There are even keyguards now available for use with iPads for those who have difficulty with the touch screen.

It is never too late to learn an appropriate method of communication. Larry Bissonnette, who along with Tracy Thresher was featured in the movie *Wretches and Jabberers,* is a person with autism who learned how to type as an adult, and there are many others who have done so. Interestingly enough, some who have typed have since developed speech, speaking while they are typing or reading it when they are done. If a person does not have a way of communicating, we cannot know how much he understands of what is going on around him. As has been often demonstrated, often those who appear not to be listening and comprehending actually have challenges in outputting (making themselves understood), not in understanding what we are telling them.

Behavior is a form of communication, and if a person doesn't have an appropriate method of communication, he will communicate through his behaviors, which is not always a good thing. I can't emphasize enough the importance of finding an appropriate system of communication to ensure a better quality of life for your loved one. The nonverbal person throwing tantrums is not doing it because it is part of his autism; he is trying to communicate something. Perhaps he is in pain and doesn't know how to communicate that in an appropriate manner. Communication is vital for self-advocacy and living a self-determined life. Sue Rubin, writer and star of *Autism Is a World,* has written about how being able to type in high school allowed her the opportunity to be involved in creating her own behavior plans. A positive behavior support plan describes what the behavior is that is affecting learning, and how it will be addressed at school. Jeremy has a few different ways of communicating. He has some verbal speech for requests, e.g., "I want cheese," but it has been hard to expand on that, although he keeps trying. He can point to written words and phrases to give responses. He usually types on a wireless keyboard attached to an iPad, or his Lightwriter (a portable text-to-speech communication aid). Recently we acquired a keyguard for the iPad so that he can type directly on that, and he is now trying it out. Sometimes he uses low-tech—a QWERTY letter board—and we have plenty of those lying around the house and in the car.

Jeremy learned to type over many years. First he learned to recognize words, understand their meaning, and then to read and to spell. When asked how he learned to read, he replies, "My mom and *Sesame Street*." From the time he was a baby I read to him on a regular basis, and I showed him picture books with word labels. He learned to name objects verbally through Discrete Trial Teaching. He learned to use "I want ..." sentences with the Picture Exchange Communication System. When he was fourteen, I started taking him for lessons with Soma Mukhopadhyay, who developed the Rapid Prompting Method (RPM) to teach her son, Tito. As explained by Jeremy in the Preface, RPM is used to teach academics with a teach-ask paradigm, and communication is taught in the process. Soma is now the educational director of HALO, Helping Autism through Learning and Outreach, based in Austin, Texas. At the time, Soma was living in Los Angeles, and we drove there twice a month (two hours each way) for a year and a half. I learned from watching Soma, and I practiced with Jeremy every day. It was slow but steady progress—no miracles here, just increasing the skill level through consistent practice.

JEREMY:

For nonverbal people with autism, behavior is a form of communication. This means that if a child leads you to the refrigerator, he is asking for food. When a nonverbal person with autism cries and hits a support person, it can mean that he is overwhelmed by the noise or lights. Nonverbal behavior is very important to the life of a person with autism for this reason.

Up until recently, my family didn't even know I was able to communicate the way I do. It was hard to get my messages through to people. If I needed to go to the bathroom or wanted to get something to eat, I had to find a way to communicate that in order to get my messages across. Both my minimal verbal and mostly nonverbal behaviors played a big role in this. If my mom didn't understand that I was hungry, I would have to grab her and bring her to the kitchen and point to the fridge.

Now that I know how to communicate better, not only can I type what I want, but I have learned to have more patience, and that can be read in my behaviors. That moment in which I realized it was time to grow up involved learning how to type to communicate, so my message skills went from pointing at objects and trying to verbalize to successfully typing letter by letter anything I had to say with whomever I wanted to.

Having autism has hindered my ability to talk, but not my ability to think. I've had a voice only since I learned to use a letter board in high school. Before I was able to communicate, I felt hopeless. Now that I can communicate, I feel hopeful. My first time communicating felt like a dream, but now it is my reality. Communication has helped my health because when I feel sick I can tell someone and ask to see a doctor. Knowing I can communicate adds happiness to my life.

People ask how I learned to type. It was lots of work. My body does not always respond to what my mind is telling it to do. People do not understand how tough it can be to get body and mind to work together.

The love that people gave me helped me initiate the supports that I need for my communication. I think that people justly freed me from my nervousness. I changed myself with the help of my support staff. They helped me take fear out of the equation by trying the strategies of RPM that Soma taught them to teach me academics.

Learning interesting information through RPM helped me under-
stand that I could have a more interesting life, so I began to change
my attitude and behaviors. I sat still and listened to people talk, and
then I developed the idea that I could talk back through writing.

The strategies that helped were repeated practice with people I
knew. Helping me to control my nerves helped. Speaking in a calm-
ing way helped, too. Initiating conversation is still very difficult. It
is hard because I can't always move my body to get my letter board or
Lightwriter or iPad.

SELF-ADVOCACY AND SELF-DETERMINATION

Self-advocacy is another important skill that is necessary and
can be taught. It begins when parents provide choices to children and then respect their choices. Self-determination is about
having control over one's life, and it is an important right that
we hold dear. Although the concept may appear to be simple,
the implementation is complex for those with a developmental
disability.

As neurotypical children become teenagers, they advocate
to stay out later, to drive the car, to go places unaccompanied by
an adult, and so on. With more freedom, they learn little by little to make (hopefully) wise choices. As parents, we give them
more responsibility for their choices because they advocate for
more control over their lives. Most teenagers on the spectrum
don't have this natural opportunity to develop self-advocacy
skills. We need to teach them, because only by learning to self-
advocate will they be able to live self-determined lives.

If your child is attending college and is over eighteen, the
college will be communicating with him or her—not you—and
your adult child will have to be able to ask for his accommodations if he requires any. At a worksite, or at a day program,
you will not be there, and your child will need to advocate for
himself to have his needs met. If your adult child is on the more
able end of the spectrum and does not disclose his diagnosis

or disability before getting hired for a job, then he will not be covered by the Americans with Disabilities Act (ADA).

Some with Asperger's Syndrome (AS) or their parents do not want to disclose that they have AS. The need for disclosure is directly related to whether or not their needs are being met. If they do not need accommodations, then disclosure is not a concern. For some, perhaps disclosure of one area of difficulty, for example auditory sensitivity, would be enough.

Self-advocacy can be taught. The first step is knowing what you want, knowing what to choose, then knowing how to ask for and get what you want or need. It's an ongoing, long-term process. The way to measure self-determination is to gauge whether your goals are being met.

For example, when doing a PATH, Jeremy identified what he wanted his life to look like in five years. Then he looked at where he would be a year from today, and then finally decided on some steps that, with the help of his family, friends, and support staff, would be taken so he would reach his goals. In this process, Jeremy is learning interdependence (i.e., asking people for help in areas they have skills) and self-determination, and he is practicing the skill of self-advocacy that he learned in high school through the IEP process.

SELF-REGULATION

Self-regulation is a necessary life skill for all facets of community life. Many on the autism spectrum have difficulty with sensory and emotional overload. One hopes this skill has been developed earlier in childhood, while receiving special education services, though for many it is an ongoing process. If they do not learn to self-regulate and to replace inappropriate behaviors with appropriate ones, it will be very hard for them to be included in society, have friends, hold jobs, attend college, and live independently or in a supported-living situation. Along with communication challenges, challenges in controlling emotional outbursts are why those on the more able end of the spectrum get in trouble with others at work and college. There is also the risk that they get in trouble with the police if they overreact in a public situation.

Although I believe it is important for society to be more accepting of people who are not neurotypical, I also realize that if a person is acting in a way that appears threatening, it can be scary and therefore is not appropriate public behavior. In saying this, it is important to realize that if a person holds it together in public, he may need to decompress at home and should be given the space to do so as long as he is not a threat to himself or others. Adults on the spectrum have explained that holding it together takes a lot of energy and can be wearying. The ability to self-regulate can fluctuate from day to day. Those living with others need to have the right and the privacy to do what they need to stay regulated at other times.

For example, Jeremy wanted to take part in a writing marathon to raise money for a nonprofit organization in San Diego. It entailed sitting in a café for nine hours with many people and writing following prompts given by moderators, as well as writing whatever he was working on at the time. I was not sure how long Jeremy would last, but it was something he wanted to do, and I figured if worse came to worst he could leave. Jeremy has never stayed in the same place that long—school was only six hours and they moved around campus. However, Jeremy did great—he participated the whole nine hours, sitting around a table with other writers. He went for two short walks, ate at the table, and did not engage in any noticeable self-stimulatory behavior, other than a very slight rocking. However, when he got home, he pulled out a piece of ribbon and was rocking and stimming away, twirling the ribbon for over an hour. It was his release for holding it together that long in public.

It is important when trying to help someone learn to self-regulate to understand the reason for the sensory overload or emotional overwhelm. Self-awareness is an important precursor for self-regulation, as the individual needs to recognize what he is feeling and realize when he is reaching his "tipping point" and to learn strategies to put into place before he hits the point of no return.

JEREMY:

I just want to tell people I want to have normal experiences, but it is very difficult. Behavioral flexibility is the ability to select an appropriate behavior to fit different communication contexts. It also refers to environmental mobility that requires a person to cope with different kinds of people in different types of circumstances. In other words, behavioral flexibility is the ability to switch our behaviors according to the settings we are in. I think behavioral flexibility is an interesting term in both the neurotypical and the autism cultures. The difference is that it comes a lot more naturally to neurotypicals because people with autism have a harder time understanding that flexibility.

Neurotypicals have behavioral flexibility. They adapt their behavior according to different factors, such as whether they are in a very small group or a large group. Neurotypical people change their behavior depending on the social group, such as whether they are in church or in a bar. Also, the group of people you are with changes your behavior.

Autistic people have many sensory-processing issues that stand in the way of being flexible. People with autism are extremely sensitive to noise, lights, and many times touch. I need direct instruction about what the rules of expected behavior are in the different environments. When I was younger, I learned the rules of going to the library. My tutors would give me the rules: Touch books nicely and keep your hands to yourself and help put the books in the red bin. If I followed the rules, I got to go for French fries; if not, I had to immediately leave the library that I loved.

SAFETY

Safety is a major concern of all parents, no matter where their adult child is on the spectrum, and their fears are well grounded, as illustrated by the statistics on pages 51–53.

Keeping young adults with autism safe is paramount. Children and adults with autism often have no sense or an underdeveloped sense of personal safety. They take risks that other children and adults do not, such as wandering from caregivers, wandering from homes, crossing streets in a dangerous manner, and being attracted to water despite not having water-safety skills. In Chapter 4, on social relationships, and Chapter 5, on dating intimacy, there are some tips pertaining to safety in regard to those specific areas.

Children and adults with autism are up to *seven times more likely* to have contact with the police and other public safety agencies. Dangerous wandering is the leading source of law enforcement contact. There is also the safety issue involving those on the more able end of the spectrum who become nervous and agitated when approached by police officers who do not recognize that the person is on the spectrum. This has ended tragically for some individuals.

Bullying is another area of particular concern that can occur at work or at college or in the community, and those who are independent in the community particularly need to learn some safety skills.

Things they need to learn, based on their ability level, include:

- Identifying and responding to safe community members such as police officers or other first responders
- Keeping an appropriate distance and not making sudden movements like putting hands in their pockets
- Carrying an ID card and an autism information card that identifies their autism, and presenting them in a safe manner
- Knowing what to do when they get lost
- Having the ability to communicate name and emergency contact information verbally and by presenting a card to a safe community member

- Identifying strangers and knowing not to interact with them
- Recognizing inappropriate touching, bullying, and inappropriate sexually suggestive behavior, and effectively reporting it to a safe person

Some topics are difficult for us parents to discuss, and one of them is the risk of physical or sexual abuse. There is a higher risk of abuse for those with developmental disabilities, although exact figures vary because of the nature of the crime. To be honest, most of us know it is out there, but we would rather not discuss it, and we prefer to believe that this is something that happens to other people. However, it is important to have the information in order to help prevent more abuse from occurring. Knowledge is empowering.

The US Department of Justice's Bureau of Justice Statistics report, based on data from the 2007 National Crime Victimization Survey, covers only those people with disabilities living among the general population in household settings; it does not cover those in institutional settings. The report stated that people with disabilities in household settings experienced violent crime at a rate one and a half times greater than people without disabilities. For females with disabilities, the rate was twice as high as women without disabilities. People with mental disabilities were most at risk. However, true figures are probably higher, as researchers working in institutional settings report extremely high rates of sexual abuse among residents.

For example, a 2003 report by Protection and Advocacy, the State Council on Developmental Disabilities, USC University Affiliated Program, and the Tarjan Center for Developmental Disabilities, UCLA, declared the neglect and abuse of people with developmental disabilities to be a public health problem for the state of California. The report stated that Californians with developmental disabilities over the age of eighteen were likely to be victimized (physically or sexually abused) four to ten times more frequently than other citizens and for longer periods of time; were at higher risk for re-victimization; and were most frequently victimized in their residences by people they know and who may be responsible for their services and supports.

Although sexual abuse among women with disabilities has long been a concern, a 2011 study published in the *American Journal of Preventative Medicine* titled "Sexual Violence Victimization Against Men with Disabilities" suggests that men with special needs are at increased risk as well. According to a 2005 survey of about 22,000 non-institutionalized adults, the prevalence of lifetime sexual violence, completed rape, and attempted rape against men with disabilities was comparable to that against women without disabilities. In the survey, nearly 14 percent of men with disabilities stated they had experienced some type of sexual violence in their lifetime compared to less than 4 percent of men without disabilities. Almost 27 percent of women with disabilities and about 12 percent of typically developing women in the survey reported experiencing sexual abuse.

Adults who have been abused can show a wide variety of symptoms, and it can be hard to distinguish abuse from other conditions. Often these signs are missed because people put these changes down to behaviors due to autism. But remember, behavior is a form of communication. Some signs could be extreme changes in behavior such as aggression, disruptive sleep patterns, toilet regression, anxiety, overactivity, becoming withdrawn, or a refusal to return to previously enjoyed locations or activities. Other signs include changes in eating or clothing preferences, or regression to a younger level of achievement and needing help in these areas. Another indication could be questions about sexuality or pregnancy that have never been brought up before. These concerns exist for men as well as women.

Research shows that often the perpetrators are individuals who have found their way into the lives of the individual as trusted care and service providers. The advice from experts is to ensure that those working with your adult child are people who have active and healthy relationships with other appropriate people, and that they have their relationship needs met outside work.

You want to make sure that the main reason people are working with your loved one is that it is their job and they are committed professionals. You do want staff persons to enjoy working with your son or daughter, but watch out for "boundary crossings" on the part of staff.

If you have any concerns, seek the help of a professional experienced in treating abuse of individuals with developmental disabilities. As well, there are Victim Compensation Boards in most states, and if your adult child qualifies they will reimburse you for trauma therapy. If something should occur, it is important that you, as a parent, also receive therapy.

There are websites listed at the end of this chapter where resources and information can be downloaded for caregivers, first responders, school personnel, and physicians on the topics of wandering, restraint and seclusion, abuse, bullying, and suicide prevention, as well as information for first responders with information and guidelines for communicating with individuals on the spectrum in emergency situations.

JEREMY:

I have oftentimes been the victim of ignorance.

I think you have to be brave to get over the horrible times people hurt you by talking like you don't understand the comments they are making about you within earshot. I don't think people realize the kind of effect they have on nonverbal people. You know that intentional abuse is unforgivable, but in some cases ignorance is just as painful.

I remember when I was in junior high the occupational therapist told the teacher I could never learn and she did not understand why I was in mainstream classes. She said I was not classroom material

because I would end up in a workshop. The teacher told her I had a
right to learn even if the occupational therapist did not agree. The oc-
cupational therapist did not get it. I was so upset because even though
I could not talk or type, I could listen and learn. I wanted to die.

I have also suffered real abuse. If it were not for my mom and
my therapist, I would have retreated into my own world. My mom
got me a great trauma therapist who helped me. It took a very long
time for me to be able to trust people again. I learned that there were
really bad people who could do things to your body, but I learned
that you don't have to let them into your soul. I feel like now I can
overcome any obstacle.

JEREMY'S TOP TEN TIPS TO PARENTS ON
FOSTERING LIFE SKILLS IN YOUR ADULT CHILD

1. **Tell your child every day that you love him.** Your child
   is being misunderstood or bullied every day. He needs
   to know that you love him and that you know he can
   understand what you are saying even if he can't respond.
   Having the knowledge you are here for him will seri-
   ously help his self-esteem.
2. **Have a good system of communication for your child.**
   People are happy when they can communicate what
   they want out of life, and this is the first step toward
   independence.
3. **All individuals need to learn how to be more independent.** Being more independent benefits everyone because the loved ones who care for us are happier when
   they have more time for themselves.
4. **Freedom to make choices is very important.** Having the
   freedom to make choices can help your adult child have
   more control over their own life. Having the opportunity
   to make choices helps people grow.
5. **Teach your child self-advocacy.** Adults need to be able
   to ask for help if they need it. I have a hard time with

my motor planning, so this is difficult for me because I cannot always get my communication devices by myself. But I keep trying.

6. **Treat your child respectfully.** Feelings can be hurt. Do not talk about your adult children in front of them unless you are including them in the conversation. Give them the respect that you give others.

7. **Have high expectations of your child.** Parents and support staff need to believe the person is smart. We should have realistic goals, but we should also have frankly high goals. If the expectations are low, so will be the results. Help them think. Rave when they work on their goals. They will dare to be great because they have your support.

8. **Goals set should be important to the person with autism and reflect his long-term plans.** Goals should be approved by the young adult before implementation. Have heartfelt, realistic goals set with the young adult. Getting their opinion is important to the individual.

9. **Teach your child to self-regulate.** My brain having autism gets me in situations where I can't think. The very best thing that helps me self-regulate is the freedom to pick my goals and work on them. Vary the choices that are given to the child of what they can choose to do. Try to help them carefully decrease the overpowering behaviors by helping them get the strength to be able to resist the temptation to get upset.

10. **Teach your child to have the courage to follow their dreams.** Tell them every day that they are smart. Very sadly, people might tell them that they are retarded. They need to know their parents know better.

GENERAL LIFE SKILLS RESOURCES:

Asperger's from the Inside Out: A Practical and Supportive Guide for Anyone with Asperger's Syndrome, Michael John Carley

Author website, Chantal Sicile-Kira, www.chantalsicile-kira.com

Autism College.com, www.autismcollege.com

Autism Life Skills: From Communication and Safety to Self-Esteem and More—10 Essential Abilities Every Child Needs and Deserves to Learn, Chantal Sicile-Kira

Life and Love: Positive Strategies for Autistic Adults, Zosia Zacks

Taking Care of Myself: A Hygiene, Puberty and Personal Curriculum for Young People with Autism, Mary Wrobel

RESOURCES ON SELF-ADVOCACY:

The Integrated Self-Advocacy ISA Curriculum: A Program for Emerging Self-Advocates with Autism Spectrum and Other Conditions, Valerie Paradiz

Ask and Tell: Self-Advocacy and Disclosure for People on the Autism Spectrum, edited by Stephen Shore

RESOURCES ON COMMUNICATION:

An Asperger Dictionary of Everyday Expressions, Ian Stuart-Hamilton

Enabling Person-Directed Planning for Augmentative and Alternative Communication (AAC) Users, http://connectability .ca/2011/06/12/enabling-person-directed-planning-for -augmentative-and-alternative-communication-aac-users/

The Hidden Curriculum: Practical Solutions for Understanding Unstated Rules in Social Situations, Brenda Smith Myles, Melissa L. Trautman, and Ronda L. Schelvan

Institute on Communication and Inclusion at Syracuse University, http://soe.syr.edu/centers_institutes/institute_communication _inclusion/default.aspx

Movie, *Wretches and Jabberers,* http://www.wretchesandjabberers.org/

Movie, *Autism Is a World,* http://www.stateart.com/works .php?workId=27

Rapid Prompting Method, www.halo-soma.org/

Sue Rubin, http://www.sue-rubin.org/

The Golden Hat Foundation, http://www.goldenhatfoundation.org/

RESOURCES ON SAFETY:

Autism Speaks Safety Project, www.autismsafetyproject.org/
Diverse City Press, http://www.diverse-city.com/video.htm (has
    some training videos and books on victimization and abuse)
National Autism Association, www.autismsafety.org

CHAPTER 4

SOCIAL RELATIONSHIPS

Friendships, Shared Interests, and Enjoyment

I get very nervous when I think about my life in the future as an adult. I am afraid that I will be all on my own with no friends.

—Jeremy

On his nineteenth birthday, Jeremy let me know for the first time that he was unhappy with his birthday presents. When I asked him why, he spelled, "I want a cell phone." "What do you want with a cell phone? You are nonverbal!" I exclaimed. "I want to text my friends," he replied. He saw how adept his younger sister, Rebecca, was at connecting with her friends via texting, and he was hoping to do the same. We got him a cell phone, but the letter and number keys were too small for Jeremy. When the iPad came out, Jeremy could use it to send emails, and it was much easier for him to communicate with people. He could access his Facebook much easier as well. Then he got his new Lightwriter, and it has texting possibilities.

All these technological advances are useful, but it doesn't guarantee that he will have more relationships.

Having friends is Jeremy's number one priority, yet it is the hardest to achieve. He joined a church youth group, took some theater classes, joined a local gym, took a staff position on the college newspaper, recently joined a community writing group, and has participated in autism conferences. He hopes that by taking part in activities he enjoys he will make some friends. At the very least, he is spending time doing something he enjoys.

Jeremy has made it clear that he wants to be fully included. He is not interested in Special Olympics or segregated activities for disabled people. It's not always easy, but we have found some activities based on his interests. Yet this area continues to be one of great difficulty for Jeremy. His real friends are the tutors or support staff whom he has known over the years. It goes to show you that if people are around long enough, they get to understand and love the person. But that is hard to find on a regular basis in the community when you have a hard time doing expected social things, such as giving eye contact while speaking. You can't blame others for not knowing about autism and not being able to tell that Jeremy is interested in forming a relationship when he is not giving out the expected social cues.

JEREMY:

I need relationships in my life, like all people do. But creating relationships is hard. I have to say that my need for relationships is in direct contrast to my having autism. My relationship experience is based on the relationships I have with my support staff who then become friends.

Having friends can make life easier for people. My support person Dana has known me for a long time, and she has told me that only friends can truly understand the person within. Like Dana says, friends are an important part of every person's life. I think that my real friends have been my support staff. Really the thing is, I need to have the understanding of my fellow citizens in order to make friends.

SOCIAL RELATIONSHIPS

There is nothing worse for parents than to see their child friendless, especially when you know they want friends. We all know people who have no romantic or love partner, and although that is sad, it is not as awful as being friendless. For those for whom social relationships are difficult, friendship is the most difficult. You can't force someone to want to be your friend or to reciprocate, and you have no control over other people's behaviors or feelings.

All parents wish for their children to have friends and a social life, and those of us with children on the autism spectrum are no different. There is a perception that because individuals with autism have challenges in the area of communication and social skills, they are not interested in having friends. This is not so. Adults with autism may be socially isolated, but it is not always indicative of a preference for solitude.

There are different reasons why adults with autism have difficulty in making friends and maintaining the friendships. Those on the more able end may have difficulty figuring out all the social cues, the necessary social exchanges, and the concepts of friendship. As well, they are usually not big on pointless chit-chat (and who can blame them?). If they have been bullied in the past, or failed at having relationships when in school, they may be afraid to try again. People tend to gravitate toward what they are good at, so if trying to connect with other people has been difficult, they will go back to their solitary pursuits. More-over, they are at risk of making naïve social decisions because of the nature of the challenges they experience.

Some adults with autism report sensory and movement challenges that can affect their ability to make friends. They may have unwanted vocal, verbal, and physical tics and nonfunctional movement that they cannot control. The differences they exhibit may lead others to assume that they are not interested in participating or communicating or maintaining a friendship. For example, Jeremy often has difficulties initiating movement. Sometimes he cannot get a verbal "hello" out, or initiate the movement to use his assistive technology device. Other times he can. He has explained many times in the past that he tells his body to move but it doesn't always respond. Observers who don't know him may think he is rude or not understanding of the social niceties that are expected, but that is not the case.

There are a few things that need to occur for our loved ones to have more relationships. First, they must learn some social skills and competencies—especially so for those who are independent and often on their own, so that they will not become victimized by others and can make some connections. Second, for those who require it, they need to have support staff who understand movement differences and sensory challenges and how to include a nonverbal person who uses alternative means of communication. Last, but not least, for friendship to occur, people need to have an open mind, be more flexible, and be more accepting of people with differences.

RESEARCH ON SOCIAL INTERACTION

Although there is a lot of research on the effectiveness of different types of social skills training for verbal children, there is not that much out there on the effectiveness of teaching social skills to verbal adults on the spectrum. The little that is out there, however, is quite clear: social skills training in groups helps develop comfort and confidence in social interactions, teach some basic skills, and reduce social anxiety. As well, it appears that the social skills groups helped by offering individuals the opportunity to meet peers experiencing the same challenges.

A review of research literature indicates that because people with autism behave, communicate, and participate in ways that are not the norm, their partners are required to be more flexible and open than usual in interpreting meaning and intention. Perceptual, sensory, and movement differences also contribute to stress and misunderstanding. People may assume that because a person focuses his attention or uses his body differently, he does not care to participate or communicate and does not desire to form a relationship. These assumptions affect our expectations of them, the way we speak with them, and the social opportunities we offer to them.

In terms of actually taking part in recreational or social activities, research concerning adults living at home with their families indicated that there was a low prevalence of having friendships, peer relationships, and participating in social and recreational activities. It appears that individuals who were younger and had less impairment in social interaction skills had more peer relationships. Those who participated more in social and recreational activities had greater functional independence, less impairment in social interaction skills, and more inclusion in integrated settings while in school.

NECESSARY COMPONENTS TO SOCIAL RELATIONSHIPS

The good news is that many people can learn and improve their social competence as they get older. Temple Grandin is a great example of this. Over the past fifteen years there has been a real improvement in her ability to navigate social situations, as observed at autism conferences and book signings. People who need assistive technology to communicate can develop social relationships if they have the right supports.

Social relationships develop based on a few necessary components, which are not easy for our loved ones, but which we can teach:

- **Communication skills:** These include verbal messages (words), paraverbal messages (how we say the words), and nonverbal messages (body language) in order to send clear messages, and to correctly understand messages someone is sending us.
- **Social skills:** These involve the ability to interact with others in a given social context in specific ways, and the knowledge and ability to use a variety of social behaviors that are appropriate to a given interpersonal situation and that are pleasing to others in each situation.
- **Social competencies:** This refers to the emotional, social, and cognitive skills and behaviors that are needed for successful social adaptation and effectiveness.
- **Interdependence:** To be interdependent means to be dependent on others for some needs. Interdependence includes knowing how to ask for help and judging who is best to ask.

One area that is difficult for many on the spectrum is understanding the "hidden curriculum," the unwritten rules of social behavior that most of us take for granted. An example of a hidden curriculum is the rules when using a public restroom. Anyone entering a public restroom will head for the empty stall or urinal that is farthest from the occupied one. Anyone, that is, except a person on the spectrum. Another example is when someone you don't know greets you with "How are you doing?," they really aren't interested in hearing anything other than "Great, thanks!"

Breaking the hidden rules of conduct can make a person seem odd, which is why it is important to teach these rules while a child is growing up. However, it is never too late, and there are a few resources at the end of this chapter to help you.

Creating social stories that include the expected rules of behavior in certain situations and places can be helpful for those of all abilities. Jeremy has asked us to remind him of the rules of behavior (which he composes himself with the input of staff) each time he goes somewhere, as it helps him stay focused on what the expectations from others are in that environment.

THE DIFFICULTIES OF MAKING FRIENDS WITH NEUROTYPICALS

JEREMY:

Neurotypicals value communication behaviors that people with autism find difficult, such as eye contact and reading body language. Neurotypicals value eye contact as a sign of respect and a way of connecting. But eye contact for a person with autism can be very difficult. I can't use my vision processing and my auditory processing at the same time. Many people with autism have this challenge, called monochannel. Not looking at a person makes it easier for me to process what they are saying.

Before I had vision-processing therapy, it was scary when unfamiliar people moved near me. When they moved their arms, I just saw blobs coming toward me. I could not tell how close they were to me. I heard Donna Williams, Ph.D., a person with autism and author of many books—including Somebody Somewhere *and* Like Color to the Blind—*speak at a conference on autism about her visual perception at different stages of her life. As I listened to what she was explaining, I realized that she and I have a lot in common. She talked about "object blindness" (the inability to recognize objects or analyze spatial relationships), and I figured out that what I knew as Picasso-like faces and blob objects all my life was the same thing as what she was describing. I felt very excited to know that there was somebody else out there who knew and understood what I saw like. Having a neurotypical friend explain expected social behaviors is necessary for my success in social situations. My circle of support teaches me to self-regulate so that I can stay in public places and not bother the neurotypicals who may feel a bit uncomfortable with my behavior.*

Relationship cultivation is about being able to connect with a partner in a way that fulfills them and is positive. People with autism do not cultivate relationships in the same way as neurotypicals. To the neurotypical, it appears as if the relationship with the person with autism is nonexistent. In a society of neurotypicals, relationship cultivation is about being friendly and showing concern. For most people with autism, relationship cultivation is practiced through shared interests. This means that we discuss facts and topics of interest. Temple Grandin is interested in animals, autism, and writing books. When my mom and Temple have a conversation, they usually discuss those topics even though they have been friends for some time.

I share different interests with different people. I like to go to the gym with Mark, Troy, and Ted, but with Laura I prefer to spend time at cafés. With Samantha I like to look at nice shops and with Dana I like to go to dinner. I like to go to the beach with Dusty. I enjoy going to Matt's to play music together and walk around his downtown area with my dog, Handsome.

Research on children with disabilities concludes that they are not able to start relationships because they do not initiate communication in the same way as nondisabled children. The neurotypicals who work with disabled children are usually quick to label them, without giving them the opportunity to show their diverse approach to relationship building. For example, children with autism like to play alongside other children but not to interact physically or verbally with them. Neurotypicals think this means they are not developing a relationship. But this is how good friends with autism begin to get used to each other.

Life is too hard to behave normal all the time. Just the other day my mom told me I should learn to behave more neurotypically because then I would make more friends. This attitude is truly not great—insisting I behave in a way that makes no sense to me. This illustrates the hopelessness of trying to be your own person because this means you must behave like everyone else to be accepted. Being different is not seen as a positive trait. I feel if I have to wear a different face, then I will attract people I don't care to know.

Different Relationships: Casual versus Close Friends

When it comes to social competencies, it's important to ensure that our adult children understand the difference between casual friends and close friends. This is important for safety reasons as well as social customs. Explaining who is a superficial or casual friend—the postal person who delivers the mail, your coworkers, the waitress at your local diner—is important. So is defining what types of conversations are "safe" to have with casual friends. These include the weather, TV shows, sports, movies, and concerts. It's important that they understand that casual friends are not the ones you talk to about sex, your financial situation, or family problems, and it is usually best to avoid religion and politics as well.

Explain to them that close friends know each other very well. They feel very comfortable with each other and can act as themselves. Sometimes a casual friend becomes a good friend over time, or sometimes it is a person you have recently met whom you click with right away. A close friend will be tolerant and understanding of your quirks, and you can discuss topics of a more private nature with them. For a person on the spectrum, a good friend can be helpful by advocating for the person, accommodating special needs, or providing you with necessary social information. Close friends can be welcomed into your home.

Knowing the difference between a casual friend and a close friend is necessary not just to avoid making social gaffes, but also to help keep your loved one safe. Your adult child needs to understand the rule that you do not invite casual friends into your home.

For example, Barbara, a young woman with Asperger's Syndrome, moved out into her own apartment when she was twenty-two. She had never dated and was interested in meeting someone. Barbara signed up for a dating service and began to communicate online with a few individuals. Not knowing the rules of safety, she invited a man to her home for their first date. Barbara was raped and her apartment ransacked by the man. Besides having this horrific experience, she had a difficult time proving to the police that she had been attacked, as she had willingly let him into her home.

A few years ago, we were shopping at our local grocery store, and when I went to pay, the checkout person and I started discussing a sporting event that had been on TV the night before. Back home, Jeremy spelled out something about my "friend at the store," and I asked him who he was talking about. He spelled, "the lady you paid for the food." I explained that she was not a friend, and Jeremy explained that he thought she was because we spent time talking. I explained that she is a shop clerk we see sometimes when we shop at the store, and that she is nice and we can talk about general things. Jeremy replied, "She is not a friend, but she acts friendly." It was a great way to put it. This came in handy when he got a Facebook account, as he was wondering how people he didn't know could be "friends" on Facebook. I told him that the people he doesn't know are not really friends; they are just friendly. I knew he understood the concept.

Friendships: Rules and Expectations

JEREMY:

Last night I dreamt that I had my own home and I had a party. My home was nicely decorated in blue and other colors. I served tasty food and champagne for my guests. There were twenty guests and they were all my friends (support staff past and present) that I know only because of my autism. These are the only relationships I have been able to build. I told them how important they were in my life. I made my friends happy by telling them verbally that the big important thing they had in common was that they did not judge me by the neurotypical standard of being like everyone else.

I have to say that my life is boring in terms of the number of relationships I have. The idea that you matter in someone's life is what makes a relationship important. People must feel that there is a reason that they need to go through studying and working.

Your adult child needs to understand that friendships are based on expectations and exchanges. This means there is giving and taking on both sides. For those who do not initiate easily, like Jeremy, but who want to have friends, it is important to prompt them to remember people on their birthdays or if they are feeling lonely to contact someone by email (for example) to have an exchange. You want to make sure they understand the basic rules of friendships. Explain that a connection is made because people are interested in each other. They exchange information about an assignment in class, a favorite place to eat, or other things in common. How much is shared and what is shared depends on whether it is a casual friendship or a close friendship. Again there are different expectations implied in friendship that need to be made clear to those on the spectrum. Close friendships take nurturing. Nurturing is done by being polite, by not flaking out on a friend, by calling ahead of time and apologizing if you have to cancel or reschedule, and by helping each other from time to time. As well, friendships are like plants and need nurturing with an occasional phone call or email and by doing activities together.

It's important to explain that sometimes friendships end when one of the persons is no longer interested in keeping it up. It may be that your friend is just very busy with work or school or family life, but if time goes by with no phone calls, it's best to check in with the person to try to connect. If they are not interested anymore, it is sad but just a part of life that everyone has to deal with at one time or another. As well, your adult child needs to know what kind of people to steer away from. They should be told that if a person treats them badly (and give concrete examples), they need to stay away from them and tell a trusted adult what has happened.

The Importance of Friendships with Peers on the Spectrum as well as Neurotypical Peers

JEREMY:

Making friends to have fun with is one of the hardest parts to figure out in my life.

Recently, my mom took me to an autism conference. I met a beautiful girl with Asperger's Syndrome. She really understands my autism. We email each other a lot to discuss how being on the spectrum can make life hard, but also how our autism helps us feel music more intensely. We are going to play drums together. Blaze is a good friend on the spectrum. He knows how to help me with my communication so we can hang out without a support person at home. Sometimes we talk about girls and our college classes. Sometimes we go to the beach or out to eat.

People on the spectrum that I know and interviewed for *Autism Life Skills* discussed the importance of having relationships with people on the spectrum, as well as with nonautistic peers. Being exposed to a variety of people with autism is important because not all people on the spectrum are the same. Just because they share a label does not mean they will have anything in common or want to spend time together.

In some cities there are opportunities for people on the spectrum to get together. There are chapters of self-advocacy organizations such as GRASP listed in the resource section. As well, there are online chat rooms and groups, although it's important for the adult to be aware of the safety issues concerning sharing information online or creating relationships. For those who already spend a lot of time online, perhaps finding computer classes or clubs where they actually meet in person would facilitate the formation of some relationships.

Colleges may be a good place to find ways to interact with other peers. For example, The Spectrum Club is a registered club with the Student Activities Office at Indiana University. The members are young adults on the autism spectrum only, at the request of the members. They made it clear that they needed a space to be and feel themselves without worry of ridicule. However, on occasion neurotypical peers have been invited. At one meeting, the topic of communication issues was explored, and the faculty advisor, Marci Wheeler, invited neurotypicals so they had an opportunity to spend fifteen-minute intervals "practicing" interaction with these neurotypical peers. There are opportunities to connect with neurotypical peers as well. In San Diego, a group of neurotypical students at UCSD have started a club for high school students on the spectrum. They meet twice a month and are matched one to one with a neurotypical college student. If opportunities don't exist in your area, consider partnering with other parents to start one. For example, Sandi Anderson and Dayna Hoff, cofounder of The Autism Tree Project Foundation, have started a buddy program between the football players at USD and children on the spectrum of all ages. This program has been very beneficial for older teens and young adults.

Choosing or Creating Activities for Fun and Friendships

Most of us establish relationships through our jobs and places of worship. As many young people with autism do not work, it is important to find other places to connect with people. It's not always easy and you can't be shy. It's necessary to put yourself out there if your adult child wants to be included in the community and wants to make friends.

The obvious is to start with whatever they are interested in doing. They will be more motivated, plus they will have something to communicate about and the focus will be the common interest and not the social skills. Many towns and cities have city-run recreational programs or adult evening classes, and those can be places to look. There are inexpensive gyms, YMCAs, and JCCs. As well, there are more and more places that are tailoring their programs to make it easier for people with autism to participate.

For health reasons, as well as recreational, it is important to help them figure out some type of exercise activity to do on a regular basis. It helps with self-regulation and depression.

Some parents are creating social activities based on shared interests that provide a place to have fun, create social relationships, and develop skills that could potentially lead to employment. A good example of this is the Autistry Studios founded by Janet Lawson and Dan Swearingen, the parents of Ian, a teenager with autism. The Autistry Studios began in 2008 as a four-student workshop and now serves over thirty students from age thirteen into mid-adulthood. They offer Build Stuff, Film, and Theater workshops. Their mission is to help teens and adults with autism (including Asperger's) and other differences become successfully independent by leveraging their interests and talents while creating a community. (For more information, go to http://www .autistrystudios.com/.)

Volunteering is another way to get to know people. With Jeremy we've tried delivering Meals on Wheels, participating in a writing marathon at a café, and presenting in a few places for autism awareness. This really hasn't generated friends, but it has created community connections. As well, Jeremy's two self-employment initiatives (described in Chapter 9 on employment) helped create connections in his community and on his school campus. More recently, being a staff writer on the college newspaper has provided opportunities to connect with people.

Picking Safe Activities

For those who live on their own, developing the skill to make safe choices is important. Zosia Zaks, author of *Life and Love: Positive Strategies for Autistic Adults*, is on the spectrum and has developed strategies for fostering relationships. She suggests safe activities to pursue with people she is interested in getting to know better. Zosia suggests having a Safe Activities List that lists activities that are safe to do that the individual enjoys. Another suggestion is to have a couple of trusted neurotypical peers that you can check with about the advisability of getting involved in an activity or not. We will be discussing more of these types of strategies in the Romance and Intimacy chapter.

How to Include a Person Who Has Sensory-Processing Challenges and Uses Assistive Technology to Communicate in Social Activities

JEREMY:

Sensory-processing challenges can affect a person with autism in a community setting. People with autism can:

1. *Get nervous in new environments because we are intimidated by the whole idea of new smells, new lights, and new sound.*
2. *Get scared by unknown/new persons because their way of moving can be scary because we don't visually process their moving limbs.*
3. *Get bothered by voices that are unfamiliar to us. We need to get used to people's voices so that it doesn't hurt our ears.*
4. *Get very uncomfortable with being touched. Neurotypical people are used to touching as a meaning of expressing love or being nice, but it's important to consider that many of us feel*

very uncomfortable with being touched due to the oversensitivity of our bodies.

Keep in mind that our senses are very sensitive so we easily become overloaded. My most important message is that you must give great consideration to first making the person just feel comfortable in his environment, before introducing more people. Steps to take when including a person with autism:

1. *Use the same meeting place. We get kind of nervous in new environments. Often we have dreams of just playing nicely in the same place because little effort is needed to remember how the place feels to us.*
2. *Use the same people (for the same reason as #1).*
3. *Nicely, quietly, and calmly be (sit/stand) next to us, but not too close.*
4. *Give us or hand us objects instead of expecting interaction.*
5. *Help us by just carefully, slowly moving near us.*
6. *Interact with us by barely making small slow movements.*
7. *Talk very low, not often.*

There are strategies to include a person with autism who uses augmentative and alternative communication (AAC) strategies and devices to communicate. The support person should:

1. *Have a variety of AAC devices—high tech and low tech—to use. It helps by having different ways to communicate because some days one way will work better than another.*
2. *Don't talk too much or too loud for the person with autism.*
3. *Offer ideas about what to talk about.*
4. *Make sure the person gets opportunities to speak, by making sure he gets invited to make comments.*
5. *Do what makes him happy—not the neurotypical interpretation of what you think would make him happy. This is the best answer.*

It has been my experience with Jeremy that it is much easier to include him in community activities in which he wishes to participate now as an adult than when he was younger. Adults tend to be more understanding and accepting of differences than teenagers. The important thing is to find a group that your adult child is personally interested in being a part of, and then acting on the assumption that he has the right to be there and that he will fit right in. As long as a person is not a danger to himself or another person, there is no reason to worry about behaviors that may appear a bit different.

For example, Jeremy loves writing and wants to make friends. We had the idea of starting a writing group in a local coffee shop, until we discovered that one already existed. Jeremy started attending that writing group, along with a few others run by the same organization and was accepted by the various groups. It's important to note that Jeremy's support staff are trained in how to include Jeremy and support him in such a way that they fade into the background and Jeremy is the one communicating and participating, not the support staff.

An important part of being accepted or included in groups or in society is the attitude of the person wanting to be included, and the support person. If they approach the situation with a comfortable attitude and act as if the individual's behavior or demeanor is perfectly acceptable, then the others will accept the individual quite willingly. That has been our observation, at least.

JEREMY'S TOP TEN TIPS FOR PARENTS ON HOW TO HELP THEIR YOUNG ADULTS FOSTER SOCIAL RELATIONSHIPS

1. **Help your child make friends.** Get involved in the community so you know the opportunities that exist for your child to connect with peers there.
2. **Having both autistic and neurotypical friends is very helpful.** Making friends who understand your challenges

is important, but having neurotypical friends helps for learning to understand them.

3. **Invite others to your home.** Make sure to provide some opportunities for experiencing social times at home.

4. **Remember that your child's relationships with others may look different.** They may just like to sit quietly and share the space with the other person. That is the first step for people like me.

5. **Plan what your child would enjoy, not your idea of fun.** Many times people plan celebrations for parties but they are too noisy for most of us with autism. If the party is really for us, have it be small.

6. **It is better if the friend can communicate directly.** Friendship is hard when you need a support person and assistive technology to communicate. The support person must be quiet and not involved.

7. **Teach your child the rules.** They need to learn that if someone asks a question in an email they need to answer.

8. **Just be aware that your single children are lonely.** They want to have more contact with nice young people. It is hard for them to initiate.

9. **Explain to your child that they need to be patient.** Explain that people are busy and it's not personal if their communications like emails are not answered right away.

10. **Meet the person your child wants to have as a friend.** You can help them decide if the person is a safe friend to have.

RESOURCES:

Global and Regional Autism and Asperger Syndrome Partnership GRASP: Chapters and online support groups, http://www .grasp.org/res_sg.htm

*The Hidden Curriculum: Practical Solutions for Understanding Unstated
Rules in Social Situations,* Brenda Smith Myles, Melissa L.
Trautman, and Ronda L. Schelvan

Life and Love: Positive Strategies for Autistic Adults, Zosia Zacks

*Socially Curious and Curiously Social: A Social Thinking Guidebook for
Bright Teens & Young Adults,* Michelle Garcia Winner

*Strategies for Building Successful Relationships with People on the
Autism Spectrum: Let's Relate!,* Brian King

*The Unwritten Rules of Social Relationships: Decoding Social Mysteries
Through the Unique Perspectives of Autism,* Temple Grandin and
Sean Barron

CHAPTER 5

LOVE AND INTIMACY

Relationships, Romance, Partnerships, and Marriage

I think it is my right to hope for the love of a woman and the happiness of a home of my own.

—Jeremy

When Jeremy started communicating about having a girlfriend and also about sex a few years ago, I avoided the topic. I was hoping that, like some of his self-stimulatory behaviors and obsessions, this one would fade away. Fat chance. As he communicated more and more about it, I realized I was going to have to find some way to help him. I approached Jeremy about seeing a therapist whom he could talk to about all this, and he agreed. The focus of the therapy sessions, from my point of view, was to help Jeremy with the skills he needed to meet people—to teach him more social skills and also help him self-regulate and have someone other than his mom with whom to discuss the sexual aspects of long-term relationships.

The therapist right away explained that a girlfriend was not something Mom could go out and get just like that. "Why not?" Jeremy asked. Didn't I get him his physical therapist, his occupational therapist, his support staff, his tutors—why couldn't I just add girlfriend to the list of things I could go out and get for him?

We continued with this therapist for a few months. Halfway through what came to be the last therapy session, Jeremy grabbed my handbag off the couch, grabbed my elbow, and steered me to the door. He had never done this before, so I was surprised yet happy to see him taking such initiative. Obviously, he had decided that it was time to go, so I asked him why he wanted to leave. He spelled out, "This is not working, Mom. We came here so I could get a girlfriend, and I don't have one yet."

I guess I have become too efficient for my son over the years. With his concrete, autistic way of thinking, he doesn't get that looking for and getting a girlfriend is not the same as fulfilling his other needs.

JEREMY:

I want a girlfriend. Like my kind mom says, I need patience and real advice from a knowledgeable person. Like, how do you find the woman of your dreams? How do you make love to someone?

I had a dream last night that I went to a nearby café often and saw the same girl. I got her to type with me. She liked my sense of humor and did not care I had autism.

My mom asked her to go to the movies with us. I liked that the girl understood I needed help. Mom was just kind of there to support me.

Being disabled is not easy but not the end, either. You very much need to have parents who will guide you. My mom is able to find good people to help me. It's important to have the nerve to be satisfied with failing before achieving success.

DIFFERENT ABILITY LEVELS, DIFFERENT NEEDS

For parents of young adults, sex is probably one of the hardest topics to think about. Let's face it, most of us parents would rather not have to deal with it. Parents who think their adult child will never be sexually active or romantically involved with another person might want to give it more thought. Even if they feel their child will never be capable of it, it is still necessary to give them basic education about sex for safety reasons so that they are not taken advantage of. There are their personal rights to consider as well.

With our neurotypical young adults, we watch from the sidelines and hope they will draw on any ethical, religious, and responsibility teaching we have taught them to make wise decisions. With our young adults on the spectrum, we are obliged to take a more active role. As one of my son's therapists told me, "Most parents don't know what is going on in their adult son's head—you are getting this insight because he needs your help, and also, being autistic it does not seem inappropriate to discuss with Mom all the details." And she is right, but thinking about your adult child having sex is even less palatable than thinking about your parents having sex: some things we really don't want to know about or even imagine.

The topic of sex is a hot one, even at autism conferences. Most of the questions people stop to ask me privately are about teenagers on the spectrum and sexuality. Many parents are relieved when they find that others have the same concerns yet are not sure where to go for help and advice. For this reason Jeremy and I are sharing our experience of trying to find information and help—this is an area that is not easy for anyone.

Thanks to the increase in the number of individuals with autism, more books have recently been published about dating and intimacy and curriculum for teaching socio-sexual concepts to teens and young adults, and these are listed in the resource section. Most of these are geared toward those on the more able end of the spectrum, though some of the material can be adapted for others. When delving into the topic of sex, we can't ignore the topic of sexual abuse. The idea of your child—no matter the age—being victimized is too horrible for words, but ignoring the fact that it happens is not going to prevent it from happening. Educating your child to be safe can help.

WHAT THE PROFESSIONALS AND RESEARCH HAVE TO SAY

Research indicates that individuals with Asperger's Syndrome have the same interests and sexual needs as the general population, although their mode of expression may be different. Individuals more affected by autism who live in residential facilities demonstrate an interest in exploring sexuality and sexual self-stimulation through their behaviors.

In other words, people with autism express either verbally or through their behaviors that they have the same interest in being sexually active and having intimate relationships with others as neurotypicals do. Just like with neurotypicals, the interest varies in intensity and in what their sexual preferences or identities are. They may be heterosexual, homosexual, bisexual, or not particularly interested in sexual intimacy.

The communication challenges faced by individuals on the spectrum only adds to the difficulties of establishing interpersonal and sexual relationships. Adolescents and adults with Asperger's Syndrome are different from neurotypicals when it comes to "reading" and understanding the thoughts and emotions of another person, and to sharing their own thoughts and feelings with another person. Sensory sensitivity, restricted interests, and interpersonal difficulties can create other barriers.

Another area of concern is the young adult who develops a crush on someone and begins to engage in obsessive behavior. They may get in trouble for stalking or may scare the person by being too insistent. Due to their lack of knowledge, some may appear to be intrusive instead of displaying normal courtship behavior, and this may be considered stalking.

Their naïveté may get them in trouble as well. Adolescents and young adults on the spectrum tend to have less access to their neurotypical peers in order to learn social and romantic skills and knowledge. They may not engage in behaviors that involve interpersonal contact, such as telephoning or asking a person out on a date. This could be due to a lack of awareness or to a lack of self-confidence.

As well, adolescents on the spectrum have less awareness of privacy issues and what is considered "private" versus "public" behavior, and this can lead to problems with people in the community as well as the law.

Even though sex is a topic that is difficult for parents, it is not an area that can or should be swept under the rug. Luckily there are more and more resources out there to help parents in their quest to educate their adult children.

Research indicates that for those with Asperger's Syndrome or high-functioning autism, socio-sexual programs offering a combination of social skills trainings and sexual education, such as the one developed by Isabelle Henault (author of *Asperger's Syndrome and Sexuality*), are effective.

According to Dr. Peter Gerhardt, director of the Organization for Autism Research, the two most important issues to address are sexual safety and social issues. Even the most impacted should learn about Circles of Comfort (who may ask you to get undressed, or who may touch you); the difference between appropriate and inappropriate touching; bathroom and locker independence; and reporting of past events such as inappropriate touching. Peer expectations and social cues are important to teach, especially to those who are out in the community. Although no research documents the use of social stories to teach sexual education to individuals with autism, Gerhardt believes that, used correctly, they could be a promising method.

WILL MY ADULT CHILD EVER MARRY OR HAVE A LONG-TERM RELATIONSHIP?

There are many people on the more able end of the spectrum who are married or in long-term relationships, and some have children. Michael J. Carley, Liane Holliday Willey, Brian King, and Stephen Shore are a few well-known advocates and authors on the spectrum who are married. Others are in long-term gay or lesbian relationships or marriages.

Tony Attwood, a well-known Asperger's Syndrome expert, says that although many people with Asperger's Syndrome have challenges in the area of relationship skills, some are able to experience romantic and eventually intimate personal relationships and can become lifelong partners. Women partners of men with Asperger's Syndrome have mentioned qualities such as quiet, kind, strong, and attentive as what attracted them to their partners. The man may be perceived as a "silent stranger" due to lack of social and conversational skills, but there is the possibility that his social naïveté and immaturity can be changed by a partner who is a natural expert on empathy, socializing, and conversation.

Adults who appeared more affected by autism in early childhood and who in later childhood progressed to be considered as having high-functioning autism are often less motivated to seek a long-term relationship. They appear more content with celibacy and being on their own. They derive their self-identity and personal value by having a successful career and being independent. For some, not having a relationship can be a positive choice.

Another consideration about intimate relationships is that sometimes there can be sensory challenges. A person may be too sensitive to touch and may not tolerate the feel of another person's bare skin on their skin, for example. Even signs of affection such as hugs can be difficult. As Jeremy says, "Hugs are difficult for me because it only feels good when I decide."

In saying that, there are many on the less able end of the spectrum who desire and want to establish long-term relationships. In these cases, it is important that the individuals have parents or other advocates who are willing to help them make good choices and create the life they dream of.

For example, Sara is a young woman with autism who lived at home, and when she was twenty-two she wanted to live in her own place. A service provider agency that provides supports to adults with developmental disabilities living on their own helped her and her mother find a two-bedroom apartment. Once they found a place, Sara was provided with direct support staff to assist her in learning daily life skills and employment skills. As she needed twenty-four-hour supervision and supports, Sara shared the apartment with a neurotypical roommate who provided the nighttime supports if she needed assistance of any kind. Meanwhile, Sara met Kevin, who has a developmental disability, and after dating for several years, Kevin moved into her apartment. Then they got married. With Kevin living with her, Sara was able to get by with only a job coach for some hours a day, but she no longer needed twenty-four-hour supports from a service provider agency. Both Kevin and Sara are very much in love and have created a loving home and the life they want with the help of their parents and the service provider.

JEREMY:

I want a relationship. I want to have someone to talk to and laugh with.

Lately I feel like I want a girlfriend.

Finding love is not easy for anyone. What I mean is that most people search for love but do not find true love. I know this because I frankly see that my aunt is not married and she is a great person. The reality is that for many, they will never find true love despite being normal.

Love for me means that someone likes my way of thinking about life and the same philosophy about living. Love is not a prisoner but it makes you realize that you care about this person more than anyone else. I might find love one day. Right now I would settle for sex.

The reason I really want a healthy relationship with a girl is I want to have real love and sex. Nearly everyone wants that. I get the feeling no one really cares about my kind of situation. The therapists are interested in doing therapy on social skills. I need more.

LOOKING FOR SPECIALIST HELP

If sexual education has not been part of your child's development so far, it's never too late to start. How and what you teach depend on your adult child's ability level and interest. To begin with, determine your comfort level in discussing sexuality and sex with your young adult. If you feel you need assistance, look for resources in your area. Some geographical locations have a few good resources; some have none. It is not always easy to find the right match for your adult child. Before seeing a specialist, consider:

- What are your adult child's language and communication skills?
- What are your adult child's abstract reasoning skills?
- Is your son or daughter hyper- or hyposensitive to visual, auditory, tactile, smell, or taste? If your young adult has sensory-processing challenges, this may affect the physical aspect of having sex and needs to be taken into consideration when broaching this topic.
- Does your adult child have any other physical challenges that could affect learning?
- Where is the youth's social and emotional age in comparison with their chronological age and intellect?

- Find a specialist who understands and respects your adult child's level of understanding, social and emotional level, and wants and needs.
- Determine where your youth is in their development and ensure that the professional has the social and emotional age-appropriate materials to use while teaching your adult child.

WHAT THEY NEED TO LEARN

Thinking ahead and being proactive are important. Remember that how you teach is just as important as what you teach. Hopefully, many of these aspects will have been addressed during the teen years. Here are some general tips:

- Ensure that your adult child learns how to make and communicate choices. If someone cannot safely and assertively request something different for dinner or what they want to wear, how can we expect them to assertively claim privacy over their body or say yes or no in a social/sexual situation?
- Allow your adult child to make honest and open choices about simple and complex issues in their lives as they are able to.
- Find someone to teach the basics of safety and hygiene if they still need help in these areas.
- Be concrete when discussing sexuality—discuss the "penis" and the "vagina," not the "birds and the bees."
- Be consistent and repetitive about sexual safety, and ensure that they are learning the social aspects of sexuality as well as the nuts and bolts.
- Make sure they understand the difference between "private" and "public" behaviors. Redirect for inappropriate behaviors, such as masturbating in public. Getting the

person into the habit of carrying a book or bag or other appropriate item when out and about is useful for keeping hands occupied.

- Teach about the different boundaries that exist for different relationships, and the appropriate types of conversation and behavior for each type of relationship.
- Teach that any area normally covered by a bathing suit should not be stared at or touched, on themselves or others, unless they are in a consensual intimate relationship, and then only in private.
- Strongly reinforce the appropriate behaviors and conversations.
- It's important that the person should be able to identify places on the body where it is appropriate to be touched by others with whom they are not in an intimate relationship.
- It's important that the person be able to tell someone when he or she is touched in an "off-limits" area of the body.

TURNING TWENTY-ONE: WHAT HAPPENS IN VEGAS ...

As Jeremy's twenty-first birthday approached, one of his support staff—an ex–Navy SEAL who is in his early thirties and a single dad—suggested that it was time for a guy trip to Las Vegas. Jeremy and I were thrilled that he suggested it, but for different reasons. I was happy because it was the first time anyone had suggested taking Jeremy on a trip that was not based on his disability. Jeremy's goal for the trip was a bit different: "I want to see naked girls dancing." It is true that Jeremy could see "naked girls dancing" in strip clubs in San Diego, but parents reading this will appreciate that, since our loved ones on the spectrum tend to have obsessive tendencies, I was not about to tell Jeremy that. Obsessions with French fries I can deal with. Let him think he has to travel to Las Vegas to see naked girls dancing.

The trip turned out to be great and provided many learning opportunities, perhaps not of the type Jeremy had envisioned. There were four guys working as support staff with Jeremy at the time, and all were excited to go. At the last minute, one had to fly to Florida for an interview, and another broke up with his girlfriend a few days before the planned trip and had to look for a new place to live. Jeremy took this change of plans badly, but it was a learning experience; not all things happen the way they are planned, even the fun ones.

The planning was more complicated than anticipated. Female staff working with Jeremy wanted to go, but they were told it was a guys-only trip. At some point, we realized that as my husband and I have conservatorship of Jeremy, one of us had to be in the same city as Jeremy, just in case. My husband elected to go, and my brother flew out from the East Coast to keep him company as they were supposed to be on the sidelines.

When they came back, Jeremy was grinning ear to ear for weeks, and the support staff guys who went with him said it was so much fun we should make this a quarterly trip in Jeremy's schedule. I did not ask any questions, except "Did you have a good time, Jeremy?" He replied, "What happens in Vegas, stays in Vegas."

JEREMY:

When I was turning twenty-one, Troy, a support person, got the idea that we should go on a guy trip to Las Vegas. I had never had a trip with just friends before, so I felt more than excited. I would go to school and all my therapies and activities, but my concentration was always just a little bit off. In the back of my head there was always Vegas. Tons of questions ran through my mind constantly: What is it going to be like? Is it going to be fun? Is it going to be too much? Am I going to be able to take it sensory-wise? Will I meet any girls? Will girls talk to me at bars? I sure had hopeful answers to all these questions, but what would really happen? All I really knew was that it would be a weekend, good or bad, that I would never forget.

The anticipated weekend was just around the corner. My excitement levels were to the ceiling, I just couldn't wait for Vegas. Everything was ready to go and ready for us. The van was rented, we booked the hotel, I even got a couple of classes from one of my tutors/ friends who was also going to Vegas, Matt, of how to play cards so I could bet in the casinos. It was a few days before the trip and I knew something was up. My mom had to break it to me. Two of the guys had to cancel. She said, "Jeremy, I have bad news, but just think it really isn't that bad. You're still going to have fun." At first I couldn't believe it, I felt so disappointed and deserted by my friends. I wanted to celebrate my birthday with them and was really looking forward to having them come on this trip.

I still had a great time. We met nice girls from Canada who had rented a limousine and took us out for a drive. My friends showed me some cool night places. I behaved like a neurotypical, but that is easy to do when the neurotypicals are behaving like teenage boys. But I also behaved like a gentleman. It was cool that Troy organized it.

MORE THAN JUST THE BASICS

What was outlined in the section "What They Need to Learn" was just the basics, and discussed sexuality as a behavior. It is important that the young adult have more information after the basics, depending on their emotional and physical maturity and chronological age as well as independence. Besides the basics, there are more lessons to teach. Just as in the neurotypical population, there are questions of sexual identity that need to be addressed. The whole idea of sexuality may be difficult for many parents, but our teens and young adults need to understand about heterosexuality and homosexuality and people's different choices. As well, if your child is interested in being sexually active, they need to be aware of the possibility of sexually transmitted diseases and AIDS, and how to protect themselves from these concerns, as well as how to prevent pregnancy. Ensuring that your young adult has a trusted medical professional they can turn to for questions such as these is reassuring, since you know they will be getting good information from a valid source. Moreover, those with sensory-processing sensitivities need to know how to communicate these to their partner.

THE FRUSTRATIONS OF TRYING TO GET PROFESSIONAL HELP

Providing the lifelong basic necessities of food, shelter, and work for your loved one with autism is a constant worry. But loving caresses, physical intimacy, love, and a relationship with someone who is with you because they choose to be, not because they are related to you, are also basic necessities—the kind you can't pay for even if you have the money. Except for maybe the sex part.

Earlier in this chapter I described Jeremy's frustration that he wasn't getting closer to getting a girlfriend after a few visits to a therapist. My frustration with trying to get professional help in this area is that it costs me money, gives me more tasks to do, and raises even more questions.

One therapist suggested that Jeremy become more active in community groups such as church, which is a good idea. She also suggested that Jeremy join an online dating group in order to practice his social skills—the art of conversing, carrying on a conversation, perhaps even flirting. In theory I agree, but it posed practical problems: Who is going to help him go online? Whom do I trust of his support persons to support him in this communication area, and to monitor that what is said or happens is appropriate for both Jeremy and the person he is communicating with while he is in the learning phase? Who is going to mentor him in this process, and where do I put it in his schedule?

That day at home, Jeremy wrote: "My therapist says I need to learn more social skills; my mom says I need to practice my communication skills, but all I really need is for someone to show me how to have sex."

When Jeremy told his psychiatrist at the time that he needed to learn about the physical aspects of lovemaking, the psychiatrist suggested that I contact a sex therapist. I asked her if she could recommend anyone locally, and she recommended that I look online. Not really helpful, in my opinion. How many sex therapists are used to working with nonverbal autistic young adults with motor and sensory issues?

On an earlier occasion I had taken Jeremy to see a counselor at an agency who was experienced in educating developmentally disabled learners on how to have safe, intimate relationships with others. I had explained in a phone call that Jeremy understood age-appropriate language, but when we got there she used baby language and images, so Jeremy did not want to stay.

One time, a court investigator came to do a biennial checkup on Jeremy's living conditions and the appropriateness of his conservatorship status. She asked Rebecca and the support person working with Jeremy about Jeremy's treatment and living conditions. Then she asked Jeremy questions about whether he was happy with his current living situation and whether he was happy to continue living with us. She asked him if he had anything else to say about his living situation. "Yes," Jeremy spelled out, "I want to know when I will be allowed to have sex."

The court investigator was surprised by his response, but it brought up a couple of good points: If I have conservatorship, at what point do I get in trouble for not allowing him to have sex (i.e., not finding him a partner), and can I get in trouble for allowing him to have sex? I asked the court investigator, and she told me that she couldn't give me legal advice. When I asked her what other families do in this situation, she said the sex question had never come up before. This left me wondering if I was the only mom concerned about this part of my son's life.

I asked the court investigator if she could tell me what she thought, and she said that just because a person is physically able to have sex and wants to do so, it does not mean that they are emotionally ready, and I agreed with her. So then I asked her, "Who decides when he is emotionally ready?" She suggested that I talk to a psychiatrist or therapist....

JEREMY:

The other day, the court investigator for my conservatorship told my mom she was responsible for my relationships, including sex. I had asked the question "When will I be allowed to have sex?" when the lady asked if I had any questions. The lady said, "Good question." But she never really answered it. Then my mom just started to ask more questions about allowing me to have sex or not. The lady said no one had asked these questions before my mom. I guess the other parents don't think it is important, just worried about things like housing and jobs. I just hope my mom will figure it out for me.

HE'S JUST NOT THAT INTO YOU: PRACTICAL SKILLS THAT NEED TEACHING

An important area to cover with your young adult (if you haven't during the teen years) is to teach how to recognize the difference between a platonic and a romantic interest. For those with obsessive or passionate tendencies, mistaking politeness or friendliness for a romantic interest can create problems.

For example, Bill has high-functioning autism and is quite social. He is very much into girls, and although he is in his early twenties, his behavior toward women resembles that of a young teenager. As well, he doesn't read social cues very well, which means he often misinterprets people's intent. His mother gave an example of the problems this can create.

They were at a restaurant, and the waitress was pleasant and smiling as she explained the special of the day and took their order. Bill came to the conclusion that the waitress liked him, and he wanted to ask her out on a date. During the meal, he continued to obsess about the waitress and how she had shown signs of liking him. Whenever she approached the table, he was certain that it was another sign she wanted to go out with him. He got up a few times to try to speak with her, interfering with her work. He did not seem to realize that the attention he was giving her not only was unwanted, but made it difficult for her to get her work done. Over the next few weeks, Bill asked his mother several times a day to take him back to the restaurant, as he wanted to see the waitress and ask her out on a date. It took a month for his mother to convince him that as a waitress, her job included acting "friendly" to all the customers she served, and that she had not meant anything special by her behavior toward Bill.

In terms of differentiating between friendship and romantic interest, ASD teens and young adults may not be able to "read" the cues from another person as to whether the interest is reciprocal. They need to have explicit instruction about indications that someone likes them as a friend, as opposed to being interested romantically.

Due to social immaturity, ASD teens or young adults may not show interest in others romantically until much later than their peers, despite their sexual maturity. It is still necessary to explain about romantic feelings, however, because others in their peer group will be displaying romantic behaviors and because they may develop these feelings as they get older. It is important to explain that if they don't have these feelings now, they may have them in the future. Such discussions with teens and young adults can help demystify the change in behavior from mainly same-sex interaction to mixed interaction, flirting, touching, and showing off for the benefit of potential girlfriends/boyfriends. It helps them make sense of what is going on around them. It's a good idea to explain some of the body-language cues they may not be understanding. They need to understand what "romantically interested" and "not interested" may look like.

INTERESTED:
- Giving strong eye contact
- Leaning forward to hear what is said
- Smiling
- Flipping or touching hair
- Laughing at your jokes
- Other person initiating conversation

NOT INTERESTED:
- Looking away
- Turning away
- Moving away
- Looking unhappy
- Having arms folded
- Not responding when talked to

DATING TIPS/INTERNET DATING TIPS

If you have an adult child who is interested in dating, you want to make sure that they know some rules about making the date a success, but also about making it a safe experience for all involved. If your adult child is meeting people online, there are even more risk factors to consider. Things you need to point out, which may seem obvious but are not always so for our loved ones, include:

- The best place to find potential dates is through mutual interests (as you would find friends), by joining clubs,

volunteering, going to events where people with the
same interests will be drawn to go.

- If you make plans to meet someone for a first date, make
the date for daytime hours in a public place, such as a
coffee shop or restaurant where you will not be alone or
secluded.
- Never invite people over to your home unless you have
known them for a certain period of time and you have
become friends.
- Do not share information online such as your birth date,
address, social security number, driver's license number,
or phone number.
- Let people you know and trust, such as a relative or good
friend, know where and when you are going on a date.
- Have a few trustworthy, neurotypical friends you can
count on to ask questions when you are unsure about the
safety aspects or intentions of a person you have met.
- Have a list of safe activities and conversations already established with the help of your trustworthy neurotypical
friends. This way you have ideas to draw from when the
time comes.

REFLECTIONS: WHERE DO WE GO FROM HERE?

I very much want Jeremy to have a lasting relationship and the
love of a good woman (as he so aptly puts it). That he is so
motivated to pursue this goal is enough reason for me to help
him—there is so little that motivates him.

When Jeremy was in elementary school, he had a wooden
puzzle of a boy that had two layers to it—one of the body parts,
and a top layer of clothes. He learned his body parts and what
pieces of clothing covered what limb. As he got older, I explained the basics about where babies come from and how they
were made.

As he got a bit older, he became interested in masturbation, and I had to teach him and strictly enforce that masturbation was a private activity that he could do only in private places, i.e., his bedroom.

Jeremy has always had girls around him—at home he had mostly female therapists and respite workers, and at school he had a number of best buddies. People called him a "babe magnet" because he always seemed to be surrounded by gorgeous females. He sometimes would get invited to go out to the movies or for ice cream, and he enjoyed their company, but he did not show interest of an intimate nature in them.

The last few years, Jeremy has regularly spoken about his desire for a girlfriend. One night recently I woke up at 3:00 A.M. to find that all the houselights had been turned on. Usually a sound sleeper, Jeremy had been making the rounds. I heard him downstairs and decided to investigate. He was looking through my husband's collection of architecture books. He found the one he was looking for—*Las Vegas: The Fabulous 50s*—and flipped it open to the section on strip clubs and showgirls. "Why are you up, Jeremy, what's going on?" I asked. "I'm thinking about girls," he replied.

Oh, how I miss the prepubescent years when Jeremy was examining the guitars in music magazines and not the beautiful models holding them. Although Jeremy has been showing an interest in females for some time, he is now communicating that guitar magazines just don't do it for him anymore.

The show that finally got his attention away from Sesame Street was *Entourage*, which is a show about how four good friends from the East Coast now living in LA try to get laid and avoid relationships in between acting gigs. There is a lot of eye candy for the guys here (and the male actors are not so bad-looking, either). Dusty, one of Jeremy's tutors, offered us the DVD of the first season as a gift. Jeremy got hooked. When asked what he liked about it, Jeremy spelled out, "*I like that they are good friends.*" So I bought him *Friends,* which I thought was a little tamer but still dealt with friendships. But after watching two episodes, Jeremy didn't want to see any more. There wasn't enough female nudity to keep his interest.

Since Jeremy kept bringing up girls, I suggested that he join Facebook and work on his communication skills, as this is important for any kind of relationship. "Do you think I will really find a girlfriend on Facebook?" he asked. "It's not that simple, but you will meet people and you can connect with others right from your home and practice communicating," I told him.

Mark, one of his tutors, suggested that Jeremy start working out. He took Jeremy to check out different gyms. Once they had narrowed down their search, Jeremy and I went to discuss membership terms. When it came time to ask questions, mine were the usual: "What is the initial membership fee? What will the monthly payments come to?" Jeremy's questions at the first place were a bit different. "Are the girls nice here?" he spelled out. "Are they pretty?"

I asked Jeremy what he wants in a girlfriend. "When I think about having a girlfriend I am thinking about sex," he explained. When I asked, "Is sex all you think about?" he replied, "That really is not the main thing. I want a relationship. I want to have someone to talk to and laugh with." Don't we all.

I have encouraged him to think about love and sex as two different things so that he understands that if he goes on a date or ever has a girlfriend, he shouldn't expect sex. On the one hand, I tell him that sex is something special to have with someone you love who you are committed to. On the other hand, I would love to be able to provide him with a paid sexual surrogate so he can experience and learn about sex, as he is very interested in this. This is easier said than done, however. What is the right thing to do, and how do you go about doing it?

We have discussed a lot about what it means to have friendships and relationships and the meaning of love and how that is different from just having sex. He is beginning to understand the complexity of how it is not that easy and that, yes, being autistic, it will be difficult. But he also understands that even without autism, having a loving, intimate relationship with another person is not a given.

I ask him, "What does love mean for you?" He answers, "Love for me means that someone likes my way of thinking about life and the same philosophy about living. Love is not a prisoner but it makes you realize that you care about this person more than anyone else." I could not have said it better myself.

When you have an adult child like Jeremy who has motor difficulties, it raises other issues about who is going to help him with the physical aspects. Will it be his girlfriend? Will they need a sex therapist in there with them? There are lots of questions and few resources, but there are more now than before.

JEREMY'S TOP TEN HELPFUL TIPS TO PARENTS FOR LOVE AND INTIMACY

1. **First you must believe in the possibility of someone loving your adult child.** It's important to have that conviction yourself in order to help make it a reality for your child.
2. **Give your adult child the opportunity to have contact with all kinds of people his or her age.** This increases the number of possible opportunities to meet the right person.
3. **Teach them how to behave in the kind of environment where they can cultivate relationships with other nice people.** Help your adult child understand how to behave in a polite manner, including respecting the personal space of others.
4. **Teach them how to have a conversation even if it is with a device or picture icons if they can't speak well.** Teach them how to converse with a person of the opposite sex.

5. Teach them to understand how to know if someone is interested in them as a friend or as a possible romantic date. The signs are not obvious to us.
6. Be open to the idea that they may want a sexual experience when they are older. It is scary for parents to think about.
7. Look for ways to have them learn about social relationships that can help them later develop. Teach them how a gentleman must treat a lady and vice versa.
8. Carefully allow them to learn about sex if they want to. Then they can truly be comfortable with the idea if they are interested.
9. Teach your child how to keep clean. Hygiene must be thought of as the top priority.
10. Remember that your happiness is very important to how your child feels about his or her situation. If you are accepting of the belief that life can be good even with autism, then they will think so, too. You are the most important person in your child's life, and you can make them believe that anything is possible.

RESOURCES

Books:

A 5 Is Against the Law! Social Boundaries: Straight Up! An Honest Guide for Teens and Young Adults, Kari Dunn Buron
The Asperger Love Guide: A Practical Guide for Adults with Asperger's Syndrome to Seeking, Establishing and Maintaining Successful Relationships, Genevieve Edmonds and Dean Worton
Asperger's Syndrome and Sexuality: From Adolescence through Adulthood, Isabelle Henault
Autism-Asperger's and Sexuality: Puberty and Beyond, Jerry and Mary Newport
Intimate Relationships and Sexual Health: A Curriculum for Teaching Adolescents/Adults with High-Functioning Autism Spectrum

Disorders and Other Social Challenges, Catherine Davies and
  Melissa Dubie
Life and Love: Positive Strategies for Autistic Adults, Zosia Zaks
*Making Sense of Sex: A Forthright Guide to Puberty, Sex and
  Relationships for People with Asperger's Syndrome,* Sarah Attwood
Mozart and the Whale: An Asperger's Love Story, Jerry and Mary
  Newport
*Taking Care of Myself: A Hygiene, Puberty and Personal Curriculum for
  Young People with Autism,* Mary Wrobel

Movie:

Adam, http://www.imdb.com/title/tt1185836/

Websites:

Diverse City Press, http://www.diverse-city.com/video.htm (has
  some videos and books on sexuality training)
Planned Parenthood: Developmental Disabilities and Sexuality
  Curriculum, http://www.plannedparenthood.org/ppnne
  /development-disabilites-sexuality-31307.htm
Speak Up: Safeguarding People Who Use Augmentative and
  Alternative Communication, http://www.accpc.ca/Speak_Up
  /resources-sexhealthk&saac.htm#7

CHAPTER 6

LIVING ARRANGEMENTS

Housing and Home Skills

I like the idea of having my own house with roommates, but I also
want to live with a woman who will make me happy.

—Jeremy

While Jeremy was growing up, there were many aspects of his future life about which I was not clear. However, I was determined that Jeremy would live in his own home with roommates of his choosing and in the community of his choosing.

I have a belief that all individuals on every dial have a right to be fully included in the community. This philosophy comes from my days working at Fairview State Hospital in Orange County (now called Fairview Developmental Center), where I prepared one of the first groups of young people severely affected by developmental disabilities to be deinstitutionalized following the passage of the Lanterman Act. We taught them self-help skills and functional living skills so that they could live in group homes.

Luckily, Jeremy is not a danger to himself or to others, and he does not wander or try to run away. Jeremy dreams of one day living in his own home. Why should he expect any less? He has worked hard on his self-awareness and his self-regulation skills, so he is a good housemate to have.

Yet we need to face the fact that Jeremy's dream might take a lot longer to accomplish. Given that he needs twenty-four-hour supports, we anticipate a high cost of staff expenses. As states reduce funding for adult services, the brunt of that cost will fall on the shoulders of the family. There will be more adults on the spectrum needing services and housing soon. Those who hope to earn a living and contribute will be challenged by how much it costs. Jeremy is on a waiting list for low-income housing. We put his name on it when he was eighteen, and we were told the wait was five years. Now he is twenty-two, and we have been informed there is another eight-year wait. There are other options, and we will pursue them.

Another aspect to consider is how to know when your adult child is ready for the move away from home. Jeremy's feeling about whether he wants to move out changes on a weekly basis. Young adults often have conflicting feelings about becoming more independent. Some days they may be adamant about having their own place and looking forward to moving out. On other days they may say they are not ready yet. It's a hard decision for both the parents and the adult child about the right timing to make that move.

Other parents may be in a situation where they cannot continue to have their adult child living at home because he needs more structure or supports than they can provide, or he is a danger to himself or others. It's never easy to ponder these issues when a crisis comes to a head, so it is better to know your options ahead of time if possible.

JEREMY:

I think parents should begin planning housing when their children are still young. Money helps buy time because it is very hard to find housing if you don't have money. In my drive to get supported living, my trust in people is helping steer the process.

I see young people who work as my support staff having the roommate dilemma of finding a place and people to share a home with. I think it will be hard for me but not impossible. I dream of someday getting my own house with roommates, but I lose sight of my dream when the daytime comes.

Many students who live at home are quietly yearning to be free from their parents but don't know how to go about it. Having to move out of your house can create fear. Facing the things you are afraid of can be challenging, hectic, yet daring and exciting. Moving out is scary because money is tight when you are a student, but this can also make you interested in becoming more independent. The fear of starting a new real life is hard, but there are really great aspects, too. Thinking of moving out can be freeing for the soul of the student who wants to be on his own.

WHAT THE PROFESSIONALS AND RESEARCH HAVE TO SAY

There is much concern about the number of teenagers on the spectrum who will soon be reaching adulthood. As mentioned in Chapter 1, 69 percent of disabled adults reportedly live with their parents or guardians. Only 17 percent live independently, compared to more than half of children with no disabilities. One study called Opening Doors, conducted by the Urban Land Institute Arizona, Southwest Autism Research and Resource Center, offered solutions and ideas on how residential housing could be created for those on the autism spectrum—from those needing minimal assistance to those needing more intense supports. Some of the problems identified by the study included a lack of consistency in the definition of residential options existing in the community and a lack of guidelines in terms of designing for those with autism. As well, access to building capital is limited and cumbersome, and there are service and provider challenges.

WHAT THOSE ON THE SPECTRUM HAVE TO SAY

When it comes to housing, there seems to be general agreement on issues such as quiet, safety, and the importance of color. For those who suffer from sensory-processing challenges and have acute hearing, living in an apartment building can be a nightmare. Hearing the noise from the other apartments upstairs and downstairs is difficult. Brian King shared that another challenge for someone like him is the fretting over the social interaction in the lobby, where neighbors stop for the required chitchat. Neighbors may knock on the door and want to hang out and talk. For those who have already many relationships they are trying to deal with—extended family, colleagues—the pressure to have more when they already have enough can be terrifying. However, the good thing about an apartment building is that if something breaks you have only one person to deal with: the super handles the problem once you tell him.

While some self-advocates in the community push for complete inclusion, others believe we need to be open to group living situations because some adults on the spectrum may need or prefer autism-specific housing accommodations. Some of the environmental features they may need include soothing colors and reduction of ambient noises. They may also need social accommodations not available in "across disabilities" housing, such as not being considered in noncompliance or depressed just because the individual does not elect to eat in the cafeteria or join social events.

The number of people in a house does not make a setting institutional. What is important is to ensure that all the factors that go into supporting true connection to community and an authentic life of purpose are present in whatever option exists.

FINDING OR CREATING THE IDEAL LIVING ARRANGEMENT

Like everything else, planning ahead and knowing what you and your adult child want are important when looking at housing. In Chapter 7, we will be discussing support staff, and it is necessary to review that information when looking at housing. In this section we cover other concerns. There are different types of residential models, and you need to choose one based on your loved one's needs. Ideally, you will be looking into this long before it is time to make a move. Consider the following:

- Setting: Does your child prefer the country or the city? Does he want to live on his own or with others? What setting will help him become more independent? Does the setting build on your child's strengths? Where would she be happiest?
- Environment: What is the least restrictive environment that your adult child could successfully live in with the right supports?
- Supports: What kind of supports does your child need? Are there medical concerns or dual diagnosis to be addressed?
- Safety: Often I hear parents discussing a rural setting for their child, and when asked why, many reply, "safety." It is important to note that being in a rural area does not mean your child is safe from the possibility of abuse. A particular environment should be chosen based on what the adult child prefers, where he is happiest, and where he will have a good quality of life.

Identify your child's needs and abilities. The supports your child will require depend on how capable he is of taking care of himself and handling all the household chores. The most important life skill to consider is self-regulation. If your child is unable to control his behaviors and is a danger to himself or others, the housing choices will be more limited.

Find out if and where your ideal setting exists. Search in your area for adult services to see what exists in line with the living arrangements you are looking for. See below for different residential options, but keep in mind that not all of them exist in every state. If you are starting early—which is a good idea—ask your local school district. State agencies can give you some information, as can parents in autism support groups and other developmental disability organizations. We all know that there are not enough spots out there. If what you are looking for doesn't exist in the area you are looking at, find out if there are others interested in the same types of options and see if you can start talking about making it a reality. Many parents are actively involved in creating housing options with other parents. Build it and they will come!

Research carefully the options you are considering. Whether you are considering a residential facility or an agency that will be providing support in a supported or independent living arrangement, research your options carefully. Please look at Chapter 7 in regard to caretakers and support staff. Here are more variables to consider, depending on the type of residential option you want:

- What is the availability of twenty-four-hour supports for emergencies or crisis situations?
- What are the supports in place for mental health issues and/or duly diagnosed adults?
- How close are they located to places important to your son or daughter (i.e., job, coffee shop, library), and how often does your child have access to them?

- How much interaction is there with the community at large?
- What kind of transportation exists?
- What activities are offered in the home and outside the home?
- How much input do the individual and family have on the hiring of support staff and on the schedule and activities that are offered, and in the plan of services?
- What is the ratio of support staff to resident? What clinical staff do they have?
- What is offered (if anything) in terms of vocational services, life skills training, adult learning opportunities?
- How is the transition facilitated from the individual's family home to his new home, and what is done to help the process be smooth for all involved?
- May the parent speak to other families with experiences with these facilities or service provider agencies?

Find out about funding options. You may need to cut through a lot of red tape, but don't be discouraged. Again, for all listed below, research through your state and local agencies, and contact local autism organizations in your area to find out any tips from parents of adults with developmental disabilities. Even if you are not sure what your child will be needing, it's good to get him or her on as many lists as possible. Here are some places to start:

- **Federal and state entitlements:** Find out what is available in your area and if your adult child qualifies. Finding the funding requires tenacity. The Housing and Urban Development website is at http://portal.hud.gov/portal/page/portal/HUD, but check with local organizations to find out how it applies in your area.
- **Private pay:** Families who have the resources may opt to partner with other parents and pool their resources.

- **Charitable organization or large donor:** Some families create and contribute to the construction/acquisition funding through a 501(c)(3) organization that serves individuals with developmental disabilities.

CURRENT HOUSING AND RESIDENTIAL SUPPORT OPTIONS

Besides reflecting upon your adult child's needs, you need to know the different types that exist and the different types of services they provide. The available living options are not defined by a person's ability to be independent, but are usually defined by a person's behavior and safety concerns (e.g., is he a threat to himself or to others?) and medical needs. Not all housing options are available in all states, but many are. Here are the different types of residential options that currently exist:

- **Transitional models:** These are intended for short-term stays of usually one month to two years, with the expressed goal of transitioning the person back to the previous environment or new residence. These models usually are for those with severe behavior disorders to provide inpatient behavioral evaluation and intervention; those who are expected to live independently once they complete the program that provides an intensive life skills course; or those who are attending colleges that provide college support.
- **Supported living programs:** These provide individualized residential services to those able to live in self-owned or leased homes in the community, and they are designed to promote full inclusion of the person in the community as they work toward their long-term personal goals. The core philosophy at work here is that anyone, regardless of current skills sets, can benefit from supported living and that programming and instruction

are directed by the resident and not by the program, which usually results in a higher rate of community integration.

- **Supervised living programs:** These provide services to individuals with more supervision and direction than might be provided in supported living programs, but less than in a group home structure. In supervised living, the homes may be self-owned or leased. These residences may be small, with usually no more than one or two adults with autism per residence, scattered throughout the same apartment building or housing complex, allowing for greater staff accessibility and oversight.
- **Group homes:** Supervised and supported congregate care facilities are in smaller, more typical homes in the community. Group homes exist in every state and are small, residential homes usually owned by the provider agency. They are located in the community and usually have eight or fewer occupants and are staffed twenty-four hours a day by trained agency staff.
- **Agricultural autism community/farmstead programs:** These farmstead programs usually combine residential living arrangements, typically in several single-family homes or individual apartments in multiunit dwellings located onsite or in nearby locations, with agricultural science and community-based employment. A few of the communities are residential only. Most offer day programs, job training, and employment both on- and off-site for adults with autism who live with their families in nearby areas.
- **Intermediate Care Facility for Individuals with Mental Retardation (ICF-MR):** This is a residential program that was established in 1971 by the federal government. The funding for this facility-based program, which includes both the facility and the support services, stays with the facility, not the person, and the programs range from

large congregate settings to those that are community based and sized much like a group home. The ICF-MR has traditionally served individuals with complex needs who are medically fragile and multi-challenged. In recent years there has been a shift away from the development of new ICF-MR facilities. The trend in newer communities is toward person-centric funding.

INNOVATIVE PROJECTS

The Opening Doors study identified some innovative projects and builders of different types of residential options. Here is a sampling that parents can research online to get an idea of what a good model looks like and incorporates:

- **The Bay Area Housing Project (California).** Hello Housing, formerly Hallmark Community Solutions, developed sixty custom-designed group homes serving three, four, or five people, each with their own bedroom. They used innovative financing techniques designed to retain ownership of the homes within the public/non-profit care system for those with developmental disabilities, including autism.
- **Marc Center of Mesa, Incorporated.** This is a large non-profit corporation in Arizona with more than thirty-five group homes. Marc Center is developing a project that combines senior housing with housing for the disabled, allowing aging parents and their adult child with a developmental disability to live near each other.
- **Tom Hom Group (THG).** THG develops single-room occupancy projects across the United States and creates inexpensive rental units in urban areas. These rental units are intended for service industry workers—for example, those who work in fast-food restaurants. Tenants are single, work nearby, and earn an hourly wage.

- **Bittersweet Farms/Bettye Ruth Kay Community Homes.** Bittersweet Farms is an agricultural community in northwest Ohio, located on eighty acres in a rural setting. They offer several choices for living arrangements as well as employment/day program options for adults with autism.

Families who have not been able to find the housing they need have teamed up with other families they know to create a group home for their children. Grant is a nineteen-year-old man with little speech. He has been living in a group home since the age of fourteen because his behaviors were such that he could no longer safely live at home with his parents and siblings. As a young boy, Grant was very active, with no sense of danger, scampering up to the top of the swing set and throwing himself off, resulting in broken bones. Grant was a "runner," meaning you could not keep him contained; he would run out in any direction given the opportunity. He managed to get out of the family home many times despite the locks and security. When frustrated, Grant can be aggressive toward himself and others. There were no group homes available, so his parents found two other families with teenage boys who also needed the same type of supports. They bought a home and found an agency to provide and supervise around-the-clock staff trained in behavior management as well as in using augmentative and alternative communication strategies (communication methods used to supplement or replace speech or writing). Grant's behaviors have improved with the right supports in place, and with spending time with his housemates as well as visiting his family.

JEREMY:

Just the other day my mom brought up the idea of moving to a place where we could live in our own little houses near each other, but separate. My mom needs help with me because I require a lot of care.

My mom is trying to get supported living (where I live in my own place with a housemate who helps me in exchange for rent).

Statewide budget cuts mean that the options for me living freely in my community are in danger. They may cut IHSS (In-Home Support Services), which helps pay for the home assistance. I would like to think that I have choices like most people. The reality is that money is a problem for many, not just for me.

I think that for most students moving out represents freedom from parents. For me it means a loss of supports that help me stay free in my community. Just needing extra supports makes the idea scary.

My own mom wishes I was out of the house so that I would have more friends. However, I talked to a few students from UCSD, and they told me that being in an apartment can be lonely. In dorms it can be easier to connect with others.

Just being the one who wants to stay home longer makes it hard for me to think about the freedoms. My sister moved out and was grateful for her newfound freedom. Rebecca moved away to college, and I get the feeling she is having fun. My mom and dad are great cooks, and when I move I will have a hard time eating so well. My mom jokes and says she will stop spending time in the kitchen if it is the thing that is holding me back. Really I can't wait to be on my own. I just know I will have a great life if I have the right supports and the job to help me pay for it all.

PRACTICAL SKILLS THAT NEED TEACHING

No matter the housing structure in which your adult child lives, what is important is making the house or residence they live in become their home. For that to occur the person must have a minimum of communication skills in order to form relationships with those he is living with or those who are supporting him. As well, developing those functional living and community skills are very important, especially for those on the more able end of the spectrum who are living on their own with no or little supports.

We have always worked hard at teaching Jeremy needed community skills such as shopping, ordering in restaurants, and using the library. At home we have worked hard on him learning chores, such as emptying the dishwasher and doing his own laundry. Self-help skills have always been a priority as well. He has come a long way, but he still has difficulty with many skills due to vision-processing, sensory-processing, and movement disorder challenges. Little by little, though, he is improving in many areas and getting more independent slowly, and this remains an important focus of Jeremy's life.

Functional skills needed in community settings have historically been divided into four different areas: travel and mobility, community skills (e.g., shopping), recreation and leisure, and financial. When determining which skills your loved one needs to learn, take into consideration the following factors: individual and family preference; age appropriateness; and your adult child's access to environments and activities.

For all, interdependence skills must be even more developed. As well, communication between people living in the home and support staff needs to be established. The home skills needed for your adult child to learn will depend on what kind of housing situation he or she is in, plus what kind of wraparound supports he or she has. If a person is living on his own with no or little supports, he will basically need to be independent in all skill areas. Here are a few tips:

Teach functional skills: When teaching new tasks, systematic instruction using applied behavior analysis (ABA) is very helpful. This entails analyzing a task, breaking the task into small steps, and then teaching each step until it is mastered. There are different prompt levels that can be used. Data is taken, and problem areas can be isolated and taught separately. Most of the current teenagers and younger children have experience with this type of teaching and learning. Visual reminders such as lists (words or pictures or both) under the control of the person living there are good ways to promote independence.

Help with organization and planning: Setting up and using a system that works for the individual is important. There needs to be some kind of organization and planning when it comes to chores and keeping the house up. If a person who will be living on their own is not very good at organizing, then it could be useful to have either a professional organizer or a person skilled in this area to come in and organize according to a person's needs and preferences, and then to organize a working schedule of chores and organizational strategies to keep the home in order. Those who live on their own with little supports especially need a system that works for them. Some ideas of lists or visual supports that can be established:

- Chart of weekly chores, including a chore priority, with chores related to sanitation, health, and safety being first.
- Prevent pile buildup by making a zone map showing what acceptable items go in each zone (for example, clothing in bedroom/bathroom zone; computer stuff in office zone).
- Painting the rooms different colors can help people remember what the different spaces are used for, which can help with keeping items in the correct room.
- List of things to remember to put in a messenger bag or purse (keys, ID, wallet, phone) or to do before leaving the apartment (lock the door). Place this on the back of the front door.
- List of important phone numbers by the phone or computer.
- Copy of his class or work schedule by his desk.
- List of reminders by the dresser, such as the following: set the alarm clock, charge cell phone, etc.

LIVING ARRANGEMENTS 117

- Automatic appointment and calendar reminders set up on mobile phone and computer.
- Have a place and system to list needed items for shopping.

HOUSEHOLD AND COMMUNITY: INTERDEPENDENCE

Sharing a home with other housemates and support staff requires developing different types of relationship skills as well as practicing interdependence. Your loved one will need to learn to share some living areas and initiate to request assistance. Living on one's own, with no support staff at all, requires a developed sense of interdependence. The individual must be able to figure things out on their own, or have developed relationships with people who can help them when they need advice on how to handle certain situations or where to buy certain items in their new neighborhood.

COMMUNICATING ABOUT HEALTH CONCERNS

Those living on their own need to know when and who to ask for help regarding health concerns. Here are some ideas about what they need to know:

- **Develop a relationship with one doctor:** For the comfort level of the individual over time, as well as to allow a doctor time to get to know the person's health, it is important to stress to the individual the importance of developing a relationship over time with the same doctor.
- **Know when it is time to visit the doctor:** People with autism can be hyposensitive to pain and discomfort and not realize when they have something that warrants a visit to the doctor—be it a broken foot or a serious illness. Sometimes they have never learned, even as young children, to tell someone else when they are unwell. Learning rules

about when to go to the doctor (e.g., if you fall and hurt yourself, when you have a fever of 102 or more, when you have a headache or stomachache that does not go away for a few days even when you take over-the-counter pain-relief medication) is important for them. It is also important for them to learn to get into the habit of scheduling yearly checkups, putting it on their calendar, and then going to the appointment.

- **Communicate during the doctor's visit:** It is helpful for the person with autism to write down ahead of time the health challenges leading to the doctor's visit. If he writes down his physical complaints before going, he can then hand the doctor the list and reply to the doctor's questions about the list.

- **Bring a friend to help you:** If the adult becomes easily overwhelmed or suffers from sensory overload, and communication shuts down when stressed, it may be helpful to have a friend accompany the person to the doctor. The friend can explain what is going on from the person's list and take notes.

- **Understand about prescription medications:** It's important that the person know how to obtain the prescriptions and be able to follow directions. Transferring information about when to take medication onto a daily calendar can be very helpful, as is arranging the medication in pill-boxes identified by the day of the week.

REFLECTIONS: WHERE DO WE GO FROM HERE?

In California, the Lanterman Act gives people with developmental disabilities the right to live at home in their communities, and the Regional Centers help the individual find the necessary resources and information, and also provide supports for adult services. Jeremy has made it clear that he is interested in supported living services. Yet the economic downturn has affected the California state budget (as in all the states), which is in turn affecting services. As well, Jeremy's thoughts on when he will be ready to move into an apartment with a roommate change from week to week. Like all young adults he is nervous about this possibility while looking forward to it.

As mentioned earlier in this book, some changes have occurred in our household. Rebecca, Jeremy's sister, went away to college and is back on breaks only. My husband, Daniel, works in LA during the week. This means that Jeremy and I live alone in the family home, which is hard considering the amount of help Jeremy still needs with his personal care and supervision. Luckily, Jeremy was eligible for IHSS and has been receiving IHSS for some years now, so I was able to hire more help for the daytime hours. We also plan to have a college student living with us who, in exchange for free room and board, will support Jeremy some evenings and assist with the end-of-the-day routine. In this way, Jeremy will get used to living with people who are not family, and perhaps the college student will become one of Jeremy's roommates in his new place. This would allow me to continue traveling for my speaking engagements.

Meanwhile, we plan to look at low-income mixed-use apartment buildings that have to put aside a certain number of units for disabled or low-income residents near us and downtown San Diego.

Another option we are considering is selling our home, the value of which has not suffered from recent economic turmoil, and buying a smaller home that has two small rental units in the back for less than what our home is worth. Still another option is for us to have our current house become Jeremy's home, with roommates of his choosing as well as support staff, and for my husband and me to move to a smaller place when Rebecca no longer feels she needs her old room available for her.

I've always liked the idea of co-housing, a type of collaborative housing in which residents actively participate in the design and operation of their own neighborhoods. Everyone has their own home, but there are shared spaces and there can also be a type of barter system in which residents exchange help in areas of need. I like the idea of different ages and types of people living together, and people trading on their strengths to help each other out.

The guiding principle is that we believe in inclusion, and we are coming up with solutions so that, even if the systems fail, we will be able to make it happen. We are open to whatever possibilities may arise, as long as they are in line with our principles.

JEREMY'S TOP TEN TIPS FOR PARENTS FOR LIVING ARRANGEMENTS

1. **Think about what is important for your child's happiness.** They need joy in their lives. If they do not like where they live, they will be unhappy. The way they feel is greatly affected by their living environment. They need a calm haven.
2. **Have staff with usually sunny dispositions.** People with autism are very sensitive to the moods of others, and if the staff person is of a cheerful disposition, then the person with autism will feel happy as well.
3. **Remember when you are choosing apartments that people with autism are sensitive to noise.** Often noises sound very loud because their hearing is very sharp. Be careful to ensure that their bedroom is very nicely overlooking a quiet place.
4. **Prioritize safety.** The neighborhood should be safe to walk around in. Be careful of the people you choose to care for and support your child. Know the signs of abuse.
5. **Realize your child needs to be as independent as possible.** Try to teach them housekeeping skills by having them be involved in household chores at home. I find it is really hard because of my motor-planning challenges, but I keep trying.

6. **If you have a roommate, learn to pick a good match.** Having the same interests is good, but having different topics to share is a good way to not get bored.

7. **House rules should be established.** The roommates need to agree on what is important to keep the place feeling like a home. Things such as noise, parties, housekeeping chores, and food rules should be discussed.

8. **Get your child used to the idea of leaving home ahead of time.** Have them visit homes they could possibly live in. It's important that they get to feel out the place because they frankly are very sensitive to their environment.

9. **Have them help you pick out the colors of their bedroom walls.** Make sure those colors are calming for them. Their bedroom should be like a retreat where they can go to relax when things are overwhelming.

10. **Provide different spaces that can be used for different activities.** The house should be very welcoming to the person. Paint the nice spaces with different colors so that they know the reason for that space.

RESOURCES

Functional Skills:

App to help teach life skills: http://lifeskillswinner.com/

Systematic Instruction of Functional Skills for Students and Adults with Disabilities, Keith Storey

TEACCH Transition Assessment Profile (TTAP) kit and manuals, http://teacch.com/publications-assessment-tools-and-teaching-materials/teacch-transition-assessment-profile-ttap-kit-and-manuals

Housing:

Advancing Full Spectrum Housing: Design for Adults with Autism Spectrum Disorders, Arizona Board of Regents, Arizona State University

Federal and state entitlements: Housing and Urban Development
website, http://portal.hud.gov/portal/page/portal/HUD

Information on co-housing: http://www.cohousing.org/

National Association of Residential Providers for Adults with
Autism, http://www.narpaa.org/

*Opening Doors: A Discussion of Residential Options for Adults Living
with Autism and Related Disorders,* a collaborative report by the
Urban Land Institute Arizona, Southwest Autism Research and
Resource Center, and Arizona State University

CHAPTER 7

SUPPORT STAFF

Needed Qualities, Skills, and Beliefs

I believe that great help from support staff provides me the very control I need. Behavior can change with the right support.

—Jeremy

Ever since Jeremy was little, we've had some type of part-time or full-time help involved in our lives—babysitters, au pairs, tutors, and behavior therapists. At school Jeremy had a paraprofessional aide (teaching assistant) who provided needed supports. It's a full-time job finding and supervising the right people. Now that Jeremy is an adult we have the help of a service provider that supervises and provides direct support staff for a part of his day. Even if Jeremy continues to live with us for a few more years, I don't want us as a family to be doing it all on our own. Who would oversee Jeremy's program if there was an emergency and something happened to me? I want other people to share responsibility for the direct support staff in his life.

While Jeremy was finishing up his last couple of years receiving special education services through the school district, he was becoming more proficient at communicating and advocating for himself. Now he can help us understand how to better support him, and he can accept more responsibility for himself. Jeremy now interviews potential support staff, and he helps to train them. He gives positive feedback and tells them when he feels they need more training.

As well, Jeremy is learning to take more and more responsibility for organizing his activities and reaching goals he has set for himself. Support staff understand they are here to support him in reaching life goals or participating in activities that he has set for himself. In terms of training staff, we share the best ways to support Jeremy. But they all bring their own personality and add something new to the process.

JEREMY:

I have worried about many things but never about support staff, because help was just given to me. My mom found staff for me. Every time I need to trust someone new it is very hard, but it is getting easier every time. It is hard to allow support staff to have glimpses into my mind. Staff members free my body by helping me move around. The great thing about staff is that they are predictable.

I have to say that more support staff understand about me since the MTV show True Life: I Have Autism *was on TV. The MTV crew captured me learning to use the Lightwriter (a device with voice-output technology) at home, at school, and in the community and planning my eighteenth-birthday party. The video portrayed my life because my difficulty in communication keeps me from making friends. The show was good because it showed I really understand even if I look like I am not paying attention, and showed my sensory-processing difficulties. This is a good video that we ask people who are interested in being hired as support staff to watch before coming to an interview. Right now we are looking*

*for a housemate to live with us for free rent in exchange for help-
ing me in the evenings. I'm lucky because my parents have room
for me and a live-in helper. Having support staff means that you
are never truly alone, which can be a good thing, but also means
that you hear people discussing you all the time. I wish my daytime
support staff did not have to talk about me every time they came
on shift. My mom is happy to help them, but I can't get organized
in my mind with people in and out.*

THE IMPORTANCE OF THE SUPPORT STAFF

"People with autism don't need wheelchairs, artificial legs,
or a guide dog. Their prosthesis is people," says Ruth Christ
Sullivan, Ph.D., a founder of the Autism Society of America
(ASA), and I couldn't agree with her more. Having good direct
support staff in your loved one's life is what makes the difference between a good life and a dismal one. People who require
twenty-four-hour supervision or support literally need other
human beings to be present every single minute of their life.
Wrap your mind around the logistics of that! Often those on
the more able end of the spectrum may be considered too "high
functioning" by the systems in place to require any type of support, yet access to someone who could coach them a few hours
a week would make all the difference in their lives. They would
have a mentor, someone to ask about social relationships, and
guidance with other functional aspects of daily life.

For people like Jeremy who need direct support staff or supervision for most of their waking hours, it is important to recognize that as the person matures from a youth to an adult, the
support dynamics need to shift from caretaking to supporting.
This is a shift that should occur slowly as your teen matures into
a young adult. They need to learn to make more decisions and
take more responsibility for their actions and decisions. This
means they need to learn how to self-advocate and communicate more with the staff. As well, they still need to continue to

learn more functional life skills from trained staff to become as independent as possible.

Exiting the school district and losing the services provided by the school district is quite a shock. It doesn't matter how well you are prepared, you are never ready for it. Parents of neurotypical children will tell you that about the loss they feel when their oldest goes off to college or leaves the nest, or when their last child leaves home. They may also worry about their adult children; especially in this new economy, their adult children may have to move back in with them. But for those of us with adult children on the spectrum who are not independent, they may leave the family home, but we will always be responsible for them until the day we die.

The point is, once school ends, those six hours of a structured program that provided supports for your child are no longer there. If your child does not have the functional ability to go away to college, hold a job, or live independently, as the parent you will be providing all the supports, or negotiating with adult services in order to get needed supports.

There is a big difference in the needs of the severely impacted young adults who require twenty-four-hour supervision and supports and those with Asperger's Syndrome. Some children have aggressive behaviors and are a danger to themselves and others, and they require around-the-clock staff who are trained in handling those behaviors.

An adult child with high-functioning autism may be able to drive and perhaps be able to live independently with some mentoring. But because of the naïveté and trusting nature of people on the spectrum, there is the constant worry that they will be victimized. For example, Robert is an academically gifted yet naïve young man with high-functioning autism who graduated high school, has attempted to take a few classes at the community college, but has not been successful with advocating for his needed accommodations and the organizational aspects of keeping up with the coursework. He has had various jobs since graduating, including working in a nursing home and at a large grocery chain. He enjoys working but has difficulties with the communication and social aspects of the job, including requesting different shifts in an appropriate and effective manner. Therefore, he does not get his requests met, and then he becomes frustrated and anxious, acts belligerent, and puts himself at risk of losing his job.

Robert has these issues despite having a job coach and a supportive family and team. Regressions in his social skills have been noted since leaving high school, as he no longer has access to the supports and training provided in school. Right now he lives with his mother, who steps in to guide him when needed. She helps him stay organized at home, but now she must move back to New Zealand to take care of her elderly parents. She is arranging to keep their condo so that Robert will have a place to live. When she leaves, she hopes that she will be able to arrange for Robert to have about six hours of independent living supports a week. Otherwise, she does not know who will help him when he needs guidance. Robert's support needs are different than those of Grant (described in the previous chapter on living arrangements), who requires twenty-four-hour supports from support staff trained in behavior management. Yet without the supports of a mentor for six hours a week, Robert could end up homeless, victimized because of his naïveté, or in trouble with the law if he lost his temper when unable to communicate his needs appropriately when feeling anxious and in a panic.

No matter how or where you get the supports your adult child needs, the most important factor is the person providing the supports, and the relationship this person has with the adult. The person could be a direct support person, mentor, tutor, job coach, and so on. What is important are the qualities and skills of the staff, and the relationship between the support person and your loved one.

If you are looking at residential housing, such as group homes, for your adult child, these options usually provide the staff as well as the housing, referred to as wraparound services. If you are looking at supported living options, you may be able to choose from different service providers, depending on what is available in your area.

If there is a service provider or agency providing and supervising staff for your adult child, ensure that the agency has the same principles as you. As well, it is important that you develop and nurture your relationship with the agency and make sure that there is good communication all around.

JEREMY:

Why I Need Support Staff

Simply, I am stuck in a body that does not function well. My body does not respond always to the commands my brain gives it. That is one of the reasons why I need support staff. My support person is like a wheelchair for someone who cannot walk because their legs do not work correctly to enable them to walk. I feel that my support staff behave as a helper to my body.

I also need their help to learn how to trust other people. When I was younger, I was badly hurt by a verbal man who was in a position of trust over a group of nonverbal teens. I get nervous now when I am with other nonverbal people. I feel they are grouping potential victims with verbal people in positions of control. This is a problem for my feelings of safety. Whenever there is a need to hire new staff, my mom makes sure I interview and feel safe with any potential hire.

My need for supports includes the need for more control over my life. If I don't have support staff, I am frankly dependent on my parents. No student who is an adult wants to have to ask parents to help them with their social life. My mom eventually wants me to leave the house. But I know she will not have me move unless I have a good circle of support staff.

WHAT PROFESSIONALS HAVE TO SAY

There is grave concern shared by professionals and parents about the ever-growing need for trained support staff, as well as their training and compensation. Typically, pay is very low, and oftentimes not enough training is provided.

Research shows that direct care staff have a direct impact on the quality of life of the individuals being supported, and that by providing staff training, on-the-job mentoring, and supports when needed, these people do better at their job. For a program to be able to provide quality services, it must be able to attract and keep qualified, professional staff. However, for most programs this has proven to be a difficult task. According to a study by the US Department of Health and Human Services in 2004, the combined annual staff turnover rate for programs serving adults with developmental disabilities is 50 percent, and some programs report an ongoing staff vacancy rate of about 10 to 11 percent. The problems include the following: salaries for residential staff are low; the work is hard, hours are long, and the prestige is limited; absence of training and supervision; and lack of any state or federal credentialing standards for adult services professionals.

Inexpensive housing can in fact be found, but unless families have confidence in the service provider, families are reluctant to allow their adult children to live an independent life until it becomes a crisis situation at home.

Currently there are no national or state accreditations for support staff, and this is considered to be one of the key challenges to adult services. Dr. Sullivan, quoted earlier, is not only a founder of the ASA, but is also the chair of government affairs for the National Association of Residential Providers for Adults with Autism (NARPAA). Dr. Sullivan authored a position paper, "The National Crisis in Adult Services for Individuals with Autism: A Call to Action," which was adopted by the board of directors of the Autism Society of America in July 2001 and updated in May 2007. In it, Dr. Sullivan discusses the concerns of the autism community. These same concerns are brought up in the Advancing Futures for Adults with Autism (AFAA) National Policy Agenda, adopted in July 2010.

Things are moving slowly in terms of recognizing direct care as a profession requiring certain training and accreditations, and deserving of decent pay and benefits.

SUPPORTS AT HOME

Many adults are still living at home because of the lack of appropriate residential options. There are different funding models in different states, and often if an adult child is living at home no supports are provided. In other states, funding is provided for in-home supports, but it is up to the parents to find the providers. In some cases, these providers are considered caretakers and are allowed to do only certain things, such as providing supervision, caretaking, and taking the person to medical appointments. Often there is no component for teaching the individual more independence skills, or enabling the person to go on social outings or to attend classes. While allowing parents respite or the ability to leave the house to work, it does not allow options for the individual on the spectrum to improve his quality of life. Research conducted by the Quality of Life Research Unit in Toronto suggests that one way of enhancing quality of life among adults with developmental disabilities would be to broaden practical and emotional support among those who live more independently. Many on the more able end of the spectrum need help with the functional and emotional aspects of living on their own. Dr. Ruth Christ Sullivan suggests that one way to help both the families and the individual would be to provide in-home support staff, including services that could benefit both the family and the growth of the individual. These services could include:

- Teaching the person needed self-help skills, such as toileting, personal hygiene, showering, making the bed, dressing, preparing meals, or doing chores.
- Training and accompanying the person during community activities such as shopping for food or clothes, attending place of worship, banking, walking, bicycle safety, going to the library, and so on.
- Finding and regularly attending community groups based on an interest the person has to help with establishing contacts and practicing the needed skills for the person to participate.
- Respite for the other family members when needed.
- Support staff for those who don't necessarily need full supports, but who need a support person for some parts of their lives. Individuals on the more able end of the spectrum may need help learning household skills for independent living or help with relationship skills. These might also include learning job interview skills, or help with organizational and planning skills such as taking notes, discussing needed accommodations with Disabled Student Services, or negotiating with instructors for homework assignments.

JEREMY:

Beliefs about autism include the way services are provided. For example, some state agencies that provide services to people with developmental disabilities, including autism, give or deny services based on misconceptions. Some neurotypicals believe that nonverbal autistic people and those with low communication skills need services or extra supports, so they receive services. However, those labeled with Asperger's Syndrome (often called an "invisible disability") may need other types of supports. But because they appear very smart academically, and can talk very well about different topics, many are not provided with any support. Yet many of the people with Asperger's Syndrome end up with no jobs because they do not have "common sense" and need help with that.

HAVING SUPPORT STAFF IN THE FAMILY HOME

If you are the one hiring the support staff for your adult child, you need to be clear on the state employment laws, and make sure you go through fingerprint and background checks. Read the tips below provided by service providers and parents on the type of person to look for and the training you need to provide. If support staff will be working in your home on a regular basis, there are different aspects to consider. Establishing clear relationship boundaries, and what the expectations are for your family and for the support staff, is important. Ensure that the support staff are not drawn into and overwhelmed by your family's life, and ensure that you are not getting drawn into their personal situations. Otherwise, there is a risk of burnout. Some of the staff may become lifelong friends, but that usually happens as a result of a healthy, professional working relationship to begin with. A great resource is Lisa Ackerson Lieberman's *A "Stranger" Among Us: Hiring In-Home Supports for a Child with Autism Spectrum Disorders or other Neurological Differences.*

GETTING THE RIGHT SUPPORTS

The supports in place depend on whether a person is being supported in their own home, as in supported living, or in another type of placement—for example, a group home. Here is what service providers have to say about getting the right supports:

- **Finding the right staff.** Good service providers look for the brightest people who are creative and resourceful and have good communication skills, multitasking skills, and a keen feel for diversity. The primary quality should be the ability to form relationships that must be flexible.

Other important qualities include the ability to make quick, sound judgments and be able to work autonomously but also as part of a group. The job is emotionally challenging, and not everyone is equipped for it. They are not getting paid much (because wages are underfunded by the government), but most are doing it because they are passionate about the work.

- **Staffing should be based on individual needs, not agency needs.** Good agencies build intentional teams around the individual being supported. The person being supported is included in the process of hiring, as are their parents or family members. People who are not comfortable with that don't take the job. The staff work for people they are supporting, and the support staff have ownership of their work because of that. Relationships are developed that can help offset the low pay.

- **Staff turnover rates can be low.** If you match the right support staff with the right individual, turnover rate is surprisingly low. Other factors include providing general training and then specific training tailored to the needs of the individual being supported.

- **The top challenge faced as a service provider is the lack of adequate funding.** Service providers are expected to manage high-quality services with not very much money. The funding is extremely low, making it hard to hire and train good staff, and it is hard work.

- **Getting the supports in place is labor intensive.** There is much negotiation about getting the funding in place from the powers that be. Beyond funding, many variables have to be coordinated at the same time, and they are all affected by the person's specific needs. A good service provider has a model based on person-centered planning. But the agency has to justify the individual's needs to those holding the purse strings (usually the government). If the government agency cannot provide the funding necessary to provide proper supports, the service provider cannot commit to providing services.

TIPS ON CHOOSING SERVICE PROVIDERS

- Prepare your child by ensuring that he learns the needed communication skills and self-advocacy skills described in Chapter 3. Ensure that he is comfortable with expressing his needs and wants to support staff.
- Choose the service provider carefully. Ask to interview the agency and its providers. Having the right fit with the agency providing the supports is important. The relationship with them is not unlike a marriage; it is serious and can be lifelong. You need to know what the values of the company are and whether your principles are the same.
- Check out agency credentials. Make sure that the agency treats the people they support with dignity and respect, provides for the health and safety of clients, and recognizes the uniqueness of autism. The agency should have as its guiding principle a presumption of competence toward the person being supported.
- Advocate for your child: you will need to negotiate with the system. Don't accept an agency you don't see eye to eye with. Don't let the system get you off track from what you know your adult child wants and needs. Look for an agency that allows your adult child and you to interview prospective staff. Find out if they hire and train staff specific to your loved one's needs. Ensure that staff are trained in using augmentative and alternative communication (AAC) strategies and devices if the person needs them. Training on safety, behavioral supports, and inclusion is also important.
- Create an Essential Lifestyle Plan (described in Chapter 2) to help your staff understand your loved one's behaviors and how to best support him. This is really helpful

not only for the person being supported but for the support staff and agency supervisors.

- It is important to strike a balance regarding your involvement. Your adult child must be allowed to develop relationships without your presence or interference, but you must be aware enough to know when there are problems since our adult children don't always speak up for themselves. Good communication, honesty, and accountability between all parties are important.

- Get familiar with housing resources in your area or where your adult child wants to live, if your loved one wants to live elsewhere than at home with you. Don't give up. Find partners to help you, such as friends, agencies that share your values, local legislators, or former educators.

- If your adult child is leaving home, don't expect letting go to be easy. You may feel relief at first, but then you may have feelings of great loss. It may be very difficult for you as the parent, but realize that this is a step your adult child needs to take in order to grow as a person.

JEREMY:

I have had great support staff. Over the years my mom has found great people and trained them with the help of other professionals. The important thing is to find the right kind of person because there are some qualities that you cannot teach. My mom looks for people who seem happy and energetic but not too hyper. During the interview at first I try to behave like an observer to see how they approach me. They must also be comfortable with my dog, Handsome. During the interview, if we feel the interviewee might be a good match, the interviewee can try some interaction. My mom shows them how to communicate with me during the interview. I train with them and if they get it, they are a good candidate.

I ask them if they have a relationship with another person because otherwise they might be too interested in me and that is not always healthy. I ask them what they like to do so we can share interests. I want to emphasize that if your interviewee is kind, but you feel there is a possibility they might be a bad person, do not let them work with your adult child even at a camp or other temporary situation. Happily at home we have had great staff.

JEREMY'S TOP TEN TIPS TO PARENTS ON CARETAKERS AND SUPPORT STAFF

1. **Kindly tell your adult child's support staff how to help him self-regulate.** Each person has different thresholds for emotions and sensory overload.

2. **Have the support staff kindly ask the needs of the adult child.** They may think they know what is best for the adult child, but that is not always true. The way to treat the adult child kindly is by asking him what he wants.

3. **Train support staff or find someone who can.** There is a way to get the support staff you need. There are resources about staff hiring that you can get. Look for them. Help support staff understand your adult child. Realize that support staff do not always know how to help your adult child. Make sure a parent or trusted person is in the house until the new support person is trained.

4. **Teach staff to be respectful.** The autistic adult thinks for himself. Great staff should always understand that. They should realize that people with autism are individuals who need to be treated nicely like individuals.

5. **Staff have to know their boundaries.** If the adult child wanted a friend, he would ask. They think he wants friends, but great friends are the ones who don't work with you.

6. **Have the support staff read books by, and see videos of, people with autism.** This book and other first-person accounts can help give them understanding of the personal experience of people with autism.

7. **Realize that communication is key.** It is necessary for creating a better life for your adult child and the support staff. Understanding your needs and your adult child's needs will help the support staff better support him.

8. **Try to keep your guiding principles.** Mind that the government does not try to put your adult child in a situation where you are dependent on service providers you might not be in agreement with.

9. **Treat your adult child's support staff respectfully.** Kindly they are your adult child's bodyguards. Treat them kindly because they create good relationships, which are essential for your adult child.

10. **Realize that your staff are going to move on.** Try to just be mindful of this. Try to nicely move on, too. Maybe they will call when they want to talk. I nicely think most of my past staff like to stay in touch.

RESOURCES:

The Foundation for Autism Support and Training Organization, http://foundationforautismsupportandtraining.org/

Jay Nolan Community Services, http://www.jaynolan.org/

National Association of Residential Providers for Adults with Autism, http://www.narpaa.org/

A "Stranger" Among Us: Hiring In-Home Supports for a Child with Autism Spectrum Disorders or Other Neurological Differences, Lisa Ackerson Lieberman, MSW, LCSW

CHAPTER 8

THE ADULT LEARNING ENVIRONMENT

College and Adult Education

Attending college has been a dream of mine since I learned to type.

—Jeremy

While Jeremy was growing up, I wasn't sure he would graduate from high school, let alone attend college. I was much more concerned about him learning to be as independent as possible, and to learn a system of communication that worked for him. When he learned to point to letters and then to type, he began to take general education classes in high school because he was interested in learning. Then his teachers and school administrators encouraged him to try to obtain an academic diploma. Jeremy passed the California High School Exit Exam, passed the necessary classes, and graduated in June 2010 with a 3.78 GPA. In January 2010, he started taking his first community college class while still finishing high school.

I became familiar with the rights and responsibilities of college students with disabilities and realized that Jeremy needed to learn how to be his own advocate as he would need to request his own accommodations. Since he was over eighteen, it was his responsibility—it was no longer mine. Jeremy now needed a good dose of self-awareness. He had to be aware of which accommodations he needed and why. He also had to learn to ask for them. Over the years in high school we provided him with opportunities for learning and honing these skills through the Individualized Education Program (IEP) process.

JEREMY:

My experience as a student with a disability is a different one at college than when I was in high school. While a student in high school may have modifications in the schoolwork (as I did for my first years in high school), in college all students are required to do the same amount of work and quality as any other student. Nicely, in college I must be able to advocate for any accommodations I need.

My first experience at my local community college with Disabled Students Programs and Services (DSPS) was with a counselor named Cathy when I signed up for my first class while still a senior at Torrey Pines High School. Cathy asked how she could help. I told her, "You can help by providing a nice teacher who is understanding about autism but who expects good work. I need time to process and a note taker and a seat near the door in case I get sensory overwhelm. I need more time for tests because I have to have the tests read to me because of visual-processing challenges, and I need more time to point or type with one finger. But I do not need lower expectations in the quality of coursework I need to complete."

I have challenges in sensory processing and in movement control, so needing a team of people in order to reach my goals is a fact of life for me. I am dependent on others for most of my needs to be met.

LEARNING AFTER LEAVING HIGH SCHOOL AND THE TRANSITION PROGRAM

Most neurotypicals continue to learn all throughout their lives, even if they are not in college or following an academic course. We attend conferences, go to adult education recreation classes. Learning is a lifetime pursuit. And adults with autism also need to continue learning when they are done with high school or the transition program. Some of them are more academically inclined than others. Many need to continue learning functional life skills. Most want to learn some employment skills so they can get a job. Our challenge is to understand how to provide them with the opportunities they need to learn.

For parents of college students with autism, the biggest challenge is to change the way we advocate on behalf of our children. College is much different from high school for many reasons. One of the most important distinctions is that in college a student is responsible for all his interactions and communication with the school personnel. But for students who received educational services under IDEA (Individuals with Disabilities in Education Act), in which parents were included in every decision, it is a huge change.

As the numbers of young adults with autism grow, so do the number of college programs offering specialized supports for students on the spectrum. As well, there are more programs being developed at community colleges around the country for students who benefit from academic instruction, but who also need vocational skill training as well as formal training in functional living skills. In these programs, the adult learners continue to have some guidance and supports while they transition to real life after leaving the school system.

For neurotypical students, high school is a time when they begin to develop social relationships at school on their own. The parents become less involved with the high school, and the student takes on more and more responsibility. However, for students on the spectrum, those social connections are often nonexistent and the parents have usually been involved for every step of their education.

Another big change in college is the increased expectations and lack of a consistent schedule. Students are expected to keep up with the homework on their own, with no modification in the workload. When they are faced with a college schedule—which is not as structured as high school, with no teacher reminders about work due, or parents allowed in meetings to help navigate the social situations as well as the academic ones—trouble often ensues.

An added complication is that some students require a full-time support person to accompany them to classes throughout the day. But who pays for that, and what is their responsibility or relationship with the school?

Expect a big adjustment period. There is a wide disparity between the type of services that different colleges provide based on their knowledge and experience with students on the spectrum. It is getting better, but parents will have to do their homework in helping their young adult find a college that is understanding of their needs.

In this chapter, we will provide some examples of programs for adult learners who need more supports as well as more life skill training. We will emphasize what to consider if you have a teenager or young adult headed to college. As well, we will discuss the interdependent and social relationship skills a college student needs to survive. Communication and organization are key to staying on top of things when you are a student. In this chapter we will explore how to best prepare students for this part of their life.

WHAT PROFESSIONALS HAVE TO SAY

Although there are no hard numbers, the track record for students on the spectrum has not been good. In the past many students on the autism spectrum have failed out of college, though some have beaten the odds and prevailed despite great challenges. Many students on the spectrum are more successful in some academic subjects than their neurotypical classmates, yet they usually have difficulty with organization and planning as well as in communicating with others.

Yet, according to researcher and clinical psychologist Patricia Howlin, Ph.D., more and more individuals with autism are now able to function independently as adults. This is a major change over past decades, probably reflecting earlier diagnosis and more effective treatments. Hopefully, with more understanding and accommodations at college, more students on the spectrum will obtain degrees and learn skills that will be useful for a future career.

Services for students with disabilities called Disabled Student Services (DSS) or Disabled Students Programs and Services (DSPS) were first set up at colleges for accommodating those with physical disabilities. They understood the accommodations needed by those who had physical limitations, such as students who were blind, used wheelchairs, or were deaf. Over the years they have become more knowledgeable about the accommodations needed to aid those with learning disabilities. Now, with more teenagers on the spectrum graduating from high school, there are more colleges and programs with a better understanding of the accommodations and social supports needed for a student on the spectrum to be successful at college.

SPECIALIZED PROGRAMS

As well, there are now more and more programs being created on college campuses every year for students in the 18–22 age bracket who need more than academics. They are all a bit different: Some of them require a high school diploma; some do not. Some are more vocational or life skills oriented. Others are geared toward academics but also offer mentoring in social and organizational areas.

Talk to your school district and transition program supervisor, other parents, social workers, the community college
district, and the Department of Vocational Rehabilitation (a
state-federal program whose goal is to assist people with disabilities prepare for, secure, retain, or regain employment) to
see what is available in your area. As these specialized programs
are relatively new, be aware that not everyone is familiar with
all the options, so you will have to be proactive in finding the
resources that exist. As in all programs being offered as solutions to your adult child's needs, caution must be taken. Please
read the sections below, "Buyer Beware" and "Beyond Brochures: Questions to Ask," when you are considering any programs. As there is so little available at this time for adults, many
families are so thrilled when a program is created that they do
everything possible to get their adult child into the program
without doing the research and asking the hard questions. As
the Buyer Beware section indicates, parents do need to carefully examine possible programs. The website Think College
has a database of programs with contact information, which
is a good place to start: http://www.thinkcollege.net/databases
/programs-database?view=programsdatabase. If a program does
not exist in your area, perhaps with other interested parents you
can find a local college willing to consider starting one. Here
are examples of different types of programs:

- **College 2 Career (C2C)** is a new program being funded
  by the California Department of Rehabilitation to support students with intellectual disabilities. It is being offered at some community colleges in different parts of
  California. The three-year program has a strong focus on
  each student's learning the skills needed to get jobs. The
  first year typically focuses on life skills and community
  preparation. The second and third year, the students attend classes and participate in various work trials, internship, volunteer, or paid employment positions on campus

or throughout the community. The goals of the program and measures for success include assisting each student in gaining and keeping a paid position utilizing their skills and interests. Here is the Sacramento City College College 2 Career (C2C) web page: http://wserver.scc.losrios.edu/~dsps/c2c.html.

- **Educational Service Center of Central Ohio** has different programs that place students in quality learning experiences with their peers beyond the walls of a high school setting. To qualify, students must have completed graduation requirements but not yet exited from high school. Here is their website: http://www.escofcentralohio.org/studentservices/programs/pages/campusbasedtransition.aspx. The different programs include:
  - **WINGS** is a two-year program using community-based work experiences to combine work and daily living skills including cooking and applied reading and mathematics.
  - **STEP** is a one- to two-year program with a concentration on community integration that teaches work and related skills three days per week.
  - **Project Plus** is a one-year program teaching self-determination and concentrating on work and related skills four days per week. This is the final transition step.
  - **ACT** is a one-year program designed for students with Autism Spectrum Disorder who have completed high school graduation requirements. The program teaches self-determination through transition planning and academic coaching.
- **OPTIONS Program at Brehm School, John A. Logan College and Southern Illinois University.** OPTIONS Program is a transitional program for students with learning disabilities who have graduated from high school, earned their GED (General Education Diploma),

or who have decided to defer graduation in order to participate in a transitional program. OPTIONS instructional programming includes academic classes offered by OPTIONS faculty, instruction in employment readiness, community college experiences, internship experiences, and speech/language therapy: http://www.options.brehm.org/index.html.

POST-SECONDARY SUPPORT PROGRAMS

In addition to specialized programs created by colleges and school districts, there is a growing number of local consultants offering supports to college students on the spectrum. A variety of services exist that liaison with post-secondary education programs, coordinate services, and provide academic tutoring, life skills and social skills training, coaching and mentoring, vocational education, job internships, and job placement. Some offer summer programs as well to prepare the student for college.

There are some nationally known for-profit organizations that offer programs in many different states as well. Their programs originally were created for other types of learners but in recent years have been marketed strongly to the autism community. Some of these programs can be very pricey.

BUYER BEWARE

To parents who feel the need for assistance after leaving the supports of IDEA, the descriptions provided by organizations and their websites sound wonderful. But as with all services, buyer beware! Most parents used to public school will not be used to the marketing tactics of the for-profit entities, and they must learn to look beyond the beautiful marketing materials and visuals on the websites to get the real story.

Parents need to be careful and ask lots of questions, not just about services that relate to their child but to the whole student population. If your child does not have a mental health concern, he may develop one or he might be developing a friendship with someone who needs help, and who may be a danger to him. What reassurances do you have that this organization has the staffing, knowledge, and oversight to ensure that the students are not a danger to themselves or others?

Keep in mind that good organizations will not mind the thoroughness of your questions about their program; in fact, they will be impressed that you have a good understanding of all the factors that come into play.

BEYOND BROCHURES: QUESTIONS TO ASK

Wendy Byrnes, who has both professional and personal experience with the search for supports for college students, presented "Beyond Brochures—Things to Consider When Moving from Secondary to Post-Secondary Programming" at the Parents Education Network conference EdRev 2010.

Wendy suggests that parents need to force themselves to ask the hard questions when considering the use of support programs. You can find a complete list of questions to consider in the article "Beyond Brochures" by Wendy Byrnes and Eileen Crumm, Ph.D., at http://autismcollege.com/library/. Here are a few basic guidelines:

- **Financial Stability**: Is the agency a nonprofit or a for-profit? Have they had any complaints or lawsuits filed against them? How stable is the funding for nonprofits? What is the cost of the program, and are there other hidden costs?
- **Staffing:** How experienced is the staff? How are they trained? Are there continued training opportunities? What's the turnover rate? What is the philosophy of the organization?
- **Application Process:** How is the student's application reviewed to decide if he/she is appropriate for the program? Is the student involved in the interview process? Find out if there is a code of behavior the student must agree to;

find out if they take students with dual diagnosis (those diagnosed with a mental health disorder as well as autism) and how mental health issues are monitored. What is the ratio of applicants to those accepted?

- **Recruitment:** Ask if there are student quotas that sites may be trying to meet; find out if consultants or admissions staff get incentives for getting students through the door; check to make sure that marketing efforts and materials presented actually match the specific services that are delivered.

- **Content of the Program:** Ask about any programming in place for students who are shy, withdrawn; find out how situations are handled if a student falters or begins to fail in school; ask about supports in place; find out what measures are in place to see if a student is showing signs of stress, and what consistent supports there are for them; find out if they are assigned a mentor.

- **Housing:** Ask about who is responsible if housing situations do not work out; find out if house rules are put into place for the students; ask whom the student calls if they have a housing-related situation.

- **Service Delivery:** Ask if someone regularly checks in to see if the student is keeping up with his homework and tutoring sessions; find out if someone is monitoring the student's well-being regularly; find out how data and documentation are done for services rendered and outcomes.

- **Outcomes:** Find out the outcomes of past students in the program; ask about those who entered to get a degree or certificate and how many accomplished that.

COLLEGE BOUND

Our First College Impressions

When Jeremy began to show interest in attending college, I started to research community colleges in our area. School administrators and educational psychologists who had experience with different community colleges were able to provide information on which community colleges were more "autism friendly."

I quickly learned that finding the right college would be a bumpy road. Two DSPS offices told me that Jeremy had to call himself, even when I explained that he was nonverbal. I asked what he should do to find out more about the services and possible accommodations. Both of them told me that he should apply, and that once he was registered, he should fill out an application for DSPS services. I explained that he wanted information about DSPS services before applying. Neither of them offered any other solution.

The two community colleges that I had been told were "autism friendly" allowed me to make an appointment for Jeremy to come in with his support person and ask them questions. They both also allowed me to come for the initial visit with Jeremy and his support person.

Stories of how different individuals have fared in colleges run the gamut from hopeful to horrific. One very smart student I know was told by his DSPS counselor that he did not believe that college was a place for the student and that he should take classes at a community college for disabled adults. Another has poor motor skills resulting in unreadable handwriting—but an English professor refused to allow him to type his work. He told the student when he handed in his typed papers that his mother must have been doing his homework for him, not believing that the student was capable of fulfilling the assignment.

Choosing professors who as Jeremy says "are understanding about autism but who expect good work" is extremely important. As more and more students with autism enter the college years, more and more college DSPS counselors are getting educated about the accommodation needs and learning challenges of students with autism.

JEREMY:

Catching the Wave from High School to College: A Guide to Transition, *available online, is a great publication designed to help students with disabilities transition from high school to college. It describes the difference between being a student in high school and being one in college. There are different rights and responsibilities for both the student and the school and college.*

In college, students must take responsibility for their own supports and must be able to self-advocate to ask for them. The student must take responsibility for asking for needed accommodations. This means that a student must have good self-awareness, good self-advocacy skills, and good communication skills—three areas that are difficult for a student with autism.

Communication is extremely difficult for a student with autism. A DSPS counselor or professor may not understand how an "invisible disability" such as Asperger's Syndrome or high-functioning autism can create challenges in learning or testing in certain ways. My friend "John" has high-functioning autism and is very verbal, but he has a hard time communicating his needs in a way that counselors and professors will understand. If the professor does not know about the difficulties of autism, John has a hard time explaining that although he is smart, he needs certain accommodations. Sensory motor issues can make handwriting very difficult, or may create overwhelm in this student when there are pop quizzes.

My experiences at college with DSPS and the professors have been very positive. Luckily, my school district prepared me by having me learn what my accommodation needs were, and had me practice self-advocacy skills. My DSPS counselor at college has been very helpful with guiding me in choosing classes and professors who are experienced working with accommodations. I have more responsibilities now for myself than when I was in high school, but all college students do and it is a necessary part of growing up.

At the beginning of this semester, I had a proctored multiple-choice and short-answer test with a new support person. I was nervous and I had trouble controlling my motor movements to point accurately to the letters on my keyboard, and even though I had extended time to take the test, I could not type fast enough, so I failed it.

I had to learn how to use the process of elimination to take multiple-choice tests because the tests are harder in college than in high school. Also, I had to practice my typing so that I could type short answers quickly and accurately so I could finish the test on time. My mom encouraged me by saying I should not worry about my grade in this class, but to focus on learning more test-taking skills, including how to better prepare for tests and faster typing that I would need for my college career. With each test I got better. I passed my last test with a high score, and I passed the class.

Difference Between High School and College

As Jeremy mentions, students have different legal rights and responsibilities in college than in high school, and it is important for parents to understand on what these are based. Until a person with a disability either graduates from high school with an academic diploma or ages out of the school district (twenty-two to twenty-five, depending upon the state), the student is protected under the Individual with Disabilities in Education Act (IDEA). After that, the student is protected under the Americans with Disabilities Act (ADA) and other laws.

A college student may sign a document allowing the release of information to the parent, but is not obliged to. The amount of contact or input a parent has is really up to the discretion of the college, with permission from the student.

One of the major differences between high school and college is that certain accommodations are possible under ADA, but modifications in the homework or coursework are not allowed. For example, in high school, a student may have been allowed to turn in a three-page term paper instead of the required five pages. In college, he would be required to do the same workload as everyone else and hand in five pages, but he may receive extended time to complete the assignment.

It's important for both the parents and the student to realize that a student who struggles in the public school setting may be protected because the school is required to serve the student, but this is not the case in college. A college does not have to serve a student who is failing or having trouble adjusting; it is up to the student to ask for and get the help he or she needs to keep up.

Taking the SAT/ACT

Most, if not all, four-year colleges require that a candidate to their school take either the SAT or the ACT. Some students on the spectrum have difficulty with test taking, and as we all know, tests are not always the best measure of intelligence and knowledge, especially for those on the spectrum. Students on the spectrum tend to do better on the ACT than on the SAT, because the ACT is much more concrete than the SAT and therefore more suited to the literal minds of these students.

Some students may need the help of experienced tutors or an educational consultant to prepare for these tests. Accommodations are available for students taking College Board tests such as the SAT, the SAT subject tests, the Advanced Placement Exams, and the PSAT/NMSQT.

Both the types of accommodations available and the requirements for obtaining the accommodations are stated on the College Board website, http://www.collegeboard.com/ssd /student/. Requirements include that there be documented evidence of a disability for at least three years prior to taking the SATs, a complete psychoeducational report for documentation, and some proof from the home school that the student has accommodations there.

Many students with disabilities receive extra time, extra breaks, or extended breaks. Other accommodations may be having a quiet setting, or using a computer for some portions of the exam if someone has dysgraphia.

Information regarding the ACT exam and accommodations and requirements can be found at http://www.act.org/aap/disab/chart.html. There are two test options available: the ACT (No Writing) for Special Testing and the ACT Plus Writing. Accommodations include more than time-and-a-half testing time and testing over multiple days.

Educational Consultants

There are educational consultants who provide services to guide students and families through the entire college application process, and they can help decide which tests the student should take and when to take them. They may also suggest tutors who can help prepare the student, give families a list of appropriate colleges to look into, and then help the student through the application and essay process.

Financial Help for Disabled Students

As for all college students looking for assistance, the search for financial aid is time-consuming but necessary. Online search engines are a good place to start. Also look into local grants or specific scholarships. Besides the usual financial aid opportunities, prospective students should look for any autism-related scholarships or grants, and those for disabled students. Here is a website that lists some, where you can begin your search: http://www.disabled-world.com/disability/finance/. Check with local and national autism organizations, and the Department of Developmental Services in your state.

The Department of Vocational Rehabilitation can provide services to college students in the form of needed equipment (e.g., laptops or help purchasing books). Restrictions apply, such as the number of units a student is taking and if he is learning skills and working toward a degree that will lead to employment. For example, Jeremy would not be eligible because he is not taking enough units each semester (typing with one finger is time-consuming), and because his goal of getting a degree in communications is not considered a degree that would lead to employment.

Choosing a College

There are some aspects of choosing a college that are the same for all students, on and off the spectrum, and those include cost, which course of study the student is interested in, and whether the student plans on going away to college or staying at home.

However, many students on the spectrum have dropped out of college due to their inability to plan for and organize the needed coursework; handle the sensory overload of a noisy campus; or ask for help from available services when needed.

With your student in mind, consider:

- Does the student need a smaller, quieter environment, as he will get lost or overwhelmed on a huge campus?
- Will he do better going all four years to the same college so he does not have to get used to two colleges?
- Will attending a community college while living at home and then transferring to a four-year college farther away be more conducive to him?
- Will the student do better attending a vocational or technical college where he will have a skill at the end of two years that will lead to a job?
- Does a cooperative education program exist in a field your student is interested in? The student would then benefit from taking academic classes while getting valuable work experience.
- Is online learning an option, or will the student be too isolated?

It is really important for the adult child and parent to find out as much as possible about the track record of a college's DSPS and professors from those who have attended. It's best to set the stage for success by attending a college where the environment will be conducive to the student's needs as well as interests.

When choosing a college, consider the following questions:

- Does the college have a clearly structured academic program?
- Does the college have a good disabilities services program with the willingness to provide accommodations and support for the student's unique learning needs?
- Is there a counseling center with support services and familiarity with ASDs?
- Because of the learning differences of ASD students, they often benefit from tutoring, organizational, and personal support services. If the college does not have experience with ASDs, are the disabilities services program and counseling center committed to providing individualized support and a willingness to learn about each student's disability and needs? On most campuses, organizational and personal support services are not offered; families and advisors may need to work together to identify ways to meet these needs.

Colleges That Are Autism/Asperger's Friendly

There are a few lists out there on colleges and Disabled Students Services and Programs that are autism/Asperger's friendly, but remember—autism is a spectrum. I have heard conflicting reviews about the same colleges from parents whose students share the same diagnosis but have different abilities and challenges. It really depends on your student's needs and learning style, as well as the individual counselor your student ends up with. As well, remember that programs do change and improve over time as they gain more experience.

With that caveat, there are a few places on the Internet to research, although some of these lists may not be all that current—consider these as a starting point for your research. You may find newer lists, as this is an area that is growing as the need is expanding. When the same college pops up a few times, it is definitely worth checking out.

- Lars Perner is a professor at USC, has Asperger's Syndrome, and is the chairperson of the Panel of People on the Spectrum of Autism Advisors to the Autism Society of America (http://www.larsperner.com/autism/colleges. htm).
- CollegeAutismSpectrum.com is the website of the authors of *Students with Asperger Syndrome: A Guide for College Personnel* (http://www.collegeautismspectrum.com /collegeprograms.html).
- *K & W Guide to Colleges for Students with Learning Disabilities Produced by the Princeton Review, 10th edition.* This guide is not specific to ASDs, but it has valuable information that can be helpful.

ACADEMIC SUPPORT AND ACCOMMODATIONS

As stated elsewhere, college students need to learn the social relationship skills to be able to get the accommodations they need. They can receive support from the disabilities services program, but they will have to be able to make decisions for themselves and talk to their professors.

The DSPS usually will fill out a form or write a letter to relevant professors, indicating that a student has a disability and may need accommodations. They may give this letter to the student to pass on to the professor, or they may send it, but in any case it is up to the student to follow through with the professor and request specific accommodations. This type of interdependence and social communication does not come naturally to those on the spectrum, and they will need coaching and support in order to do so. Some counselors are more or less willing and able to help with this; others may not be in a position to help.

Most colleges have tutorial services. It is a good idea to explore the ways in which they can help the student. The student may especially need help for the independently structured projects. The program that provides disabilities services should be able to provide information about what is available and how to access these services. Again, as students on the spectrum do not naturally ask for help, the student will need guidelines as to when and how to request services.

Here are some academic accommodations that have been helpful to students:

- A quiet environment with no distractions, and lighting that is not too bright for taking tests and for studying.
- A note taker for those who have trouble listening and writing at the same time.
- Extra time on tests.
- For nonverbal students, a variety of choice boards and keyboards to provide answers during tests and in class.
- Seating where it is best for the student in class and in lecture halls. Some professors assign seats in classrooms; others do not. Seating needs to be discussed, as for some students it can make all the difference.
- For small group projects in which students work together, talking with the professor about any challenges will be necessary. Sometimes accommodations are necessary, and at other times just having the professor's support and understanding is enough.

SUPPORT STAFF

JEREMY:

Being a student with a disability, I have found the road to being a college graduate to be long and uneven. However, the counselors in the Disabled Students Programs and Services make it possible for those who are smart and brightly able to advocate for their needs.

My communication support partners are necessary because I need help with my motor planning and my sensory challenges. Just like some people in wheelchairs need someone to push them, I need someone to help me navigate from place to place on campus, and physical assistance with setting up my communication devices. Just because I have problems controlling my movements is not a reason to deprive me of an education and a career. Having the right kind of support staff is necessary to have success in life.

Some students, like Jeremy, require a one-to-one support staff person. Again, there is a shift from the responsibility of a one-on-one paraprofessional in high school to a support person in college. In high school, the paraprofessional does much more prompting of timelines, helping the person organize his time, and communicating with the teacher. In college, the support person is there to support or assist, but under the guidance of the student. So, for example, the support person may make the phone call at the request of the nonverbal student to set up the meeting with a counselor on campus or with the professor during visiting hours when the student requests, and she may remind the student about approaching deadlines, but it is up to the student to initiate communication with the professors and counselors, and to respond in class.

This shift in thinking really takes practice. Often, people will address the support staff and not the student (especially if the student has limited verbal skills and uses assistive technology to communicate), and the support person needs to redirect all comments to the student. The student as well needs to take responsibility for initiating communication.

During Jeremy's last years in high school, we added goals in his IEP that shifted the responsibility to him for more and more direct communication with his teachers and administrative staff.

As well, we had goals for organizing and planning school projects and study time, and directing staff on research for projects. This was all very helpful in getting him used to realizing that it was his responsibility to make sure he got the work he needed done in time in order to be successful in his classes.

PARTICULAR CHALLENGES FACED BY COLLEGE STUDENTS ON THE SPECTRUM

Planning and preparing for college well in advance is important. As part of the Individualized Education Program process, each student has an Individual Transition Plan (ITP) starting by at least age sixteen. Learning the skills necessary for college (and for the world of work) should be part of this plan. Many important skills that will facilitate success in college are similar to those needed to be successful at work or for living more independently from parents. These skills can be taught and practiced, at home as well as at school, while the student is in high school.

Most of the challenges that college students on the spectrum face are related to social relationships and executive functions (planning, organizing, and problem solving). In college, the student will have to communicate on many different levels: with other students for social and study reasons and with DSPS counselors, with academic advisors, with the professors when they need help, with their one-on-one support person if they need one. Yet many on the spectrum are not used to depending on other people—being interdependent—or asking for help. But the parents will not be involved at this level, so it is important that they practice this skill before college.

Below are the areas students on the spectrum will need guidance and practice on:

- **Relationships and Perspective Taking**
  At college, there will be many more offices and people that your student will need to be in communication with

on his own—academic services, disabled student services, counseling services, tutoring services, and so on. In order to get his or her needs met, the student will need to be able to develop social relationships with them all. Perspective taking, knowledge of the "hidden curriculum" (the rules of social behavior we neurotypicals take for granted), asking for help, and negotiating to have needs met are all skills the student will need to practice before starting college.

- **Disclosure and Self-Advocacy**
  Students will have to decide how much or how little they wish or need to disclose about their autism. Disclosure is directly related to whether they need help in getting their needs met. Obviously, students requiring a support person (such as Jeremy) need to disclose this to the DSPS office, to the professor, and probably to the other students in his class.

  Those who do not require as much support but require accommodations will need to disclose to the DSPS counselor and to the professor. He may not find it necessary to disclose his actual diagnosis to other people, but he may want to let others—for example, possible dorm neighbors, or the residence hall advisor—about the challenges he has (e.g., that he is sensitive to loud noise).

  It's important that the student understand what his or her learning needs are, and the types of accommodations that are helpful. In college, he or she will probably find it helpful to talk to advisors and professors about these issues. This will be easier to do when it has been practiced in the more supportive environment of high school. At home, high school students should be learning and practicing daily living and independence skills they will need to live successfully at college, if they are leaving home.

Some areas that students need to work on during the transition program at school include:

- Understanding their disability and how it affects their learning.
- Describing their strengths and weaknesses in a clear manner that others can understand.
- Knowing what their legal rights are in regard to accessing services.
- Knowing what resources are available and how to access them.
- Developing the skills to live as independently as possible.

- **Socializing with Peers**
There are usually many on-campus social groups and activities, and there will usually be one that is in line with one of the student's interests. When the focus is on a topic of interest, the student will have less challenges with the actual social skills. He or she may need help in finding the right groups and getting introduced. Sometimes the residence advisors, service organizations on campus, or the DSPS can be helpful.

- **Structure**
There are clear differences in the structure of schedules between high school and college that make the transition from one to the other daunting. In high school, students usually attend classes Monday through Friday for usually six hours of structured time and clear-cut assignments. There is a lot less structured time in college. In high school, every day, or every other day, students have the same class at the same time and the teacher prompts the students to do their assignments and hand them in. In college, a student may have a class once or twice a week, and it is up to him to remember to do the assignments

and turn them in. If a student does not have good executive functioning skills—usually not a strong point for students on the spectrum—it will be difficult for them to stay on top of things in college.

This is a change, not only for the children, but also for parents whose children are still living at home and attending college nearby, especially if you work at home.

- **Executive Function: Organization and Planning**
By now you and your student should have a good understanding of the organizational strategies that work for him or her, and the same clear, systematic organizational strategies should be put into place to cover not only academic work, but all aspects of daily life. Visual reminders, calendars, and checklists can be developed with the student. Use of reminders on phones, iPads, and computers can be extremely helpful. It is often easier for these students to work for a short, specified period of time, and then to take a break. Using a visual timer on the computer, which shows time disappearing with a red bar that gradually gets smaller and smaller, will help him manage his work intervals on his own.

If he does not have much of a structure in place, help him create one, showing him how to schedule times for studying, school projects, and chores. Have this visible on a semester-long calendar, including all the holidays. Make sure that he schedules downtime and social/recreational activities.

A great tool for helping to keep notes organized for reviewing is the Smartpen, which records everything you write and hear in the classroom.

- **Selecting Courses**
During the first year, taking a reduced course load can be an important factor to success and keeping stress lev-

els to a minimum. Many students on the spectrum take extra time to problem solve and to complete their work and may need more time than most students to do the reading and the assignments. It's a good idea to find an academic counselor who can get to know the student and help guide him to courses that fit in with his interests and strengths and can advise on which professors would be a good match.

- **Living Arrangements**
  A big factor in picking out a college is whether the student feels capable of living in a residence hall or if he needs to stay at home. For those considering living in dorms, a single room is probably the best option. Having a roommate can be stressful. The student on the spectrum will need his own sanctuary where he can regroup, away from bright lights, noise, and social interaction. If the student is in agreement, it could be helpful to disclose to the residence staff the student's disability and areas in which support may be needed. The student may also wish to disclose to some of the students who live in adjacent rooms, so they have an understanding of why he might act a bit differently and what his strengths and interests are.

- **Everyday Living**
  If the student is living on campus or away from home, it will be helpful to the majority of them to have various guidelines, checklists, and preparations for any potential pitfalls that could happen, on campus and in his residence. Many students on the spectrum have challenges in problem solving, and situations can start spiraling into a possible school failure. For example, the washing machines in the residence hall may be unavailable due to maintenance on the day a student routinely does his

laundry, throwing him into a panic. Instead of finding a solution (go study and return to wash laundry on another day), he becomes agitated with the residence hall manager, then wastes the day writing angry letters to college administrators. Too many incidents such as these, and too many days wasted, can lead to failing out or being asked to leave. For this reason, it is important to have a counselor who's monitoring progress and can help the student look at the challenges in context. One might also start to identify patterns and write down possible solutions for recurring situations.

PREPARE, PREPARE, PREPARE

Ann Palmer, author of *Realizing the College Dream with Autism or Asperger's Syndrome: A Parent's Guide to Student Success,* suggested that parents and student put together a Resource Notebook. This notebook could be started during the summer before the student leaves for college, which is usually the time you are teaching him all he still needs to learn before starting college. Although this Resource Notebook is intended for those going to live away from home, it's a good idea to start the same kind of notebook for the student living at home to increase his independence and prepare him for living away in the future.

The Resource Notebook has different sections. Palmer suggests that there be a section to write down all the possible activities for free time—a good thing to do as students with ASD will be missing the routine of high school. Other information to include might be articles or lessons from the summer while you were preparing him for living away from home. Palmer recommends adding whatever you think would be useful, but her actual suggestions are: Contacts, Academics, Disability Services, Financial, Housing, Dining, Technology, and Leisure. Adding the contact information and names of important persons in each section (e.g., the academic advisor under

Academics) is helpful. Any pertinent information the student should have access to or remember in those areas should be placed there.

Palmer also suggests that as you are preparing with your student for daily life on campus, try to think about the various aspects of daily life there. Some examples: meal plans and their rules; where to eat at non-mealtimes; laundry; spending money; budget; using a campus ID and charge card; dorm rules; handling fire drills in the middle of the night; using communal bathrooms; learning about and participating in dorm activities; student health services; and first aid and how to take care of oneself during a minor illness (including how to get liquids and food when feeling under the weather) are all important.

Again, even if your student is living at home, you will want to start teaching him everyday life-management skills: how to use an alarm clock; email and texting; transportation; campus maps; finding restrooms; library hours and how to get help from a librarian; and medical emergencies (and non-emergencies). Spending a few days showing your student around campus and identifying all the things she needs to know (or even better, having a trusted peer do so) is very helpful.

Physical exercise is important not only for health reasons, but also to reduce stress, anxiety, and self-stimulatory behaviors.

There is more information on helping your student with daily functional living skills in Chapter 6, on housing and living arrangements, that may be helpful.

PERSPECTIVE FROM A STUDENT WITH ASPERGER'S SYNDROME

Life for a college student with Asperger's Syndrome can be different than for someone like Jeremy. In some ways it is harder because of the lack of a support person or mentor to help with areas of difficulties. Annie Hussey is a university student with

Asperger's Syndrome as well as a personal life coach and mentor for young adults on the spectrum. Annie finds college difficult because she is a perfectionist and holds herself to high standards, leading her to drop classes when she feels she is not performing to a certain standard.

Anxiety related to exam times and completing assignments means she needs to request to have her deadlines extended so she can allow herself time to get organized.

She finds that doing exams by herself in the disability office eliminates her anxiety about how she is doing compared to the other students around her, and helps her focus on the actual test.

Keeping her mental health in check has been important, and Annie has benefited from support with the disability services office in the form of weekly counseling sessions. Annie took a short break from college and spent time in psychotherapy, mindfulness therapy, and in a self-esteem group in order to gain confidence in dealing with real-life issues (a move and breakup with a boyfriend) and with anxiety. Annie believes that her anxiety is more of a challenge than her Asperger's Syndrome.

Annie finds that college can be easy because the subject material she studies is related to her special interests. She is studying psychology because she has a strong interest in pursuing a career related to autism spectrum disorders. As well, she has more friends because the peers are more mature and open-minded than in high school, where being grouped with less mature peers made her a target of ridicule and bullying, as they weren't understanding of her differences. She has met people she can share interests with who are more patient, open-minded, and forgiving.

Living in residence during a year of community college was a helpful transition for her, as was taking a university preparation course. The course was easy, but her goal for that year was to experience living away from home and to make new friends with open-minded people. Then when she entered university, her focus shifted to her academics, as she had become more comfortable out in the world.

JEREMY:

The most helpful supports at college are my support staff: having encouragement from the support staff, and having staff trained in inclusion. Learning to self-advocate while in high school was important because I knew that in college I would not be allowed to have my mom advocate for me. I had to be able to tell DSPS what the accommodations I needed were. I had to learn to type effectively and quickly in order to finish proctored tests within the extended time frame allowed. Being a student means I can keep on learning, and the best part is I can make connections with the community by going to a local college.

Lectures can be very long, but it is nice listening to a professor speak about something I am interested in. I enjoyed taking intercultural communications because it helped me learn about the difference between neurotypical and autistic communication, even though it was supposed to be about other countries' cultures.

Hearing classmates talking in class felt very good. It also made me feel sad because my first support person was not trained in inclusion and did not help me communicate with them. I think that having this bad experience made me want to get help communicating the right way. My current support person, Laura, knows how to help me make friends by having the students include me in the groups. I like small group discussion because I can hear opinions from my peers. The other classmates benefit from hearing the point of view of a non-neurotypical person. The nice thing is that they can also learn from me sometimes. I think they are nice to me, but I can tell that their view about me truly changes when they hear what I have to say.

Writing as a staff writer for the college newspaper gave me the opportunity to share my experiences. I wrote some feature articles about how autism affects my life. I have to say I enjoy the school newspaper staff meetings because they are related to my love of writing. The other writers and editors are very accepting of me. They try to include me in discussions, which is not always easy because my typing is slow. Also I need to have my communication partner help me initiate more conversations at school.

JEREMY'S TOP TEN HELPFUL TIPS FOR PROSPECTIVE COLLEGE STUDENTS

1. Learn carefully about getting organized.
2. Make sure you are well prepared for your tests.
3. Just try to find something you like to do and find a club to join.
4. Try to get Disabled Students Programs and Services to know you better.
5. Realize that the professors do not modify the work they expect from the students.
6. Identify your needs and recognize what accommodations you can ask for.
7. Practice explaining your needs so you will be able to communicate them to the DSPS counselor.
8. Select your classes wisely—a combination of courses that interest you and that will give you the necessary credits.
9. Try to pick professors who expect good work but are accepting of differences.
10. Hard work is necessary, but the dividends are great. Enjoy the learning experience.

JEREMY'S TOP TEN HELPFUL TIPS FOR PARENTS OF COLLEGE STUDENTS

1. **Teach your student to make his own decisions.** You may not always be available to give advice. He needs to take more responsibility for his everyday life.

2. **Help your student get ready for learning.** Tell him he is smart and will succeed.
3. **Ensure that he has a system to get organized.** He will need to plan ahead.
4. **Encourage your student by telling him he will be fine.** He needs to be reassured.
5. **Have time for your adult child.** The adult child may ask questions about college, and answering his questions will help the adult child begin his adventure to adulthood.
6. **Ask your adult child the questions he needs to know about selecting a class and selecting a major.** This will help him get an idea of what he really wants for himself.
7. **Ask the adult child about assignments.** He is facing a hard semester and will need the support to stay on top of everything.
8. **Make sure the adult child knows that accommodations are available to him.** This will help him with exams.
9. **Encourage him to get a school advisor.** The advisor will help the adult child through his college years.
10. **Teach the adult child how to pick an accepting teacher.** This will help him with the transition to higher education.

RESOURCES

Books:

Catching the Wave from High School to College: A Guide to Transition, edited by Carl Fielden et al., http://www.grossmont.edu/dsps/transition/transition00_default.asp

Life after High School—A Guide for Students with Disabilities and Their Families, Susan Yellin and Christina Cacioppo Bertsch

Realizing the College Dream with Autism or Asperger's Syndrome: A Parent's Guide to Student Success, Ann Palmer

Students with Asperger Syndrome: A Guide for College Personnel, Lorraine E. Wolf, Ph.D., et al.

Succeeding in College with Asperger Syndrome: A Student Guide, John
    Harpur, Maria Lawlor, and Michael Fitzgerald

Websites:

Beyond Brochures, http://autismcollege.com/library/
College Board, ACT, http://www.act.org/aap/disab/chart.html
College Board, SAT, http://www.collegeboard.com/ssd/student/
Financial Help for Disabled Students, http://www.disabled-world
    .com/disability/finance/
Going to College, http://www.going-to-college.org/overview/index
    .html
Indiana Resource Center for Autism: Academic Supports for
    College Students with an Autism Spectrum Disorder, http://
    www.iidc.indiana.edu/index.php?pageId=3417
Lars Perner's website, http://www.larsperner.com/autism/colleges
    .htm
Think College, www.thinkcollege.net

CHAPTER 9

EMPLOYMENT

Earning a Living

In high school I had two self-employment experiences. I learned that if you provide a service or product that people want or need, you will have customers.

—Jeremy

While Jeremy was growing up, I never stopped thinking about how he could earn a living, what he could do as an adult. By the time Jeremy entered high school, he was able to communicate his basic wants and needs, had learned how to act appropriately in public, and was calm and self-regulated. In fact, he spent every afternoon after school practicing his community skills. I was disappointed that the high school workability supervisor at the time said that Jeremy was not "ready" to work in the community, yet did not provide specific goals we could incorporate into his school program to teach him to be ready.

When Jeremy was a sophomore, I heard about self-employment or microenterprise for individuals with developmental disabilities. His teacher, Allan, was enthusiastic, and eventually Jeremy had two self-employment projects during high school that, coupled with the economics and marketing classes he was taking, taught him the fundamentals of doing business. Jeremy enjoyed the contact with his satisfied clients, and realized that he could earn money even if he could not get a job. This in turn did wonders for his self-esteem.

Later, Jeremy became interested in writing. He was given his own column in the high school newspaper, then became a staff writer on his community college newspaper. He has shown that he is capable of writing articles that people want to read. Earning a living from writing is of course not an easy task. But thinking as an entrepreneur and looking at the new technology and the possibilities the Internet provides us, I see there are definite possibilities. Jeremy is very clear that he wants to be a contributing member of society. As a parent, I feel it is my obligation to help him reach his goal.

JEREMY:

My early experiences with work were with my mom and school teacher. When the workability supervisor at the school district told them I was not ready for the community, they decided to create a job for me. They figured out a way for me to earn money based on my teacher's realization that there was a market not being met: teachers could not leave campus for lunch. I took orders and delivered sandwiches that I got from a health food store for a dollar less than I sold to the teachers.

The next year I put together flowers I bought at a wholesaler and sold them at lunchtime to students. I learned about the cost of doing business and profit and loss. I made enough money to get my assistance dog, Handsome. My mom made me pay for the costs of everything for doing my business. I even put in a bid to do the flowers for a wedding, and I got the job. I paid the support staff and driver to help me and I still made a profit.

THE REALITIES OF EMPLOYMENT

People work for a variety of reasons, the most important being money. However, for people on the autism spectrum, a workplace may be the only place where they have contact with people and an opportunity to develop relationships other than with family members or residential staff.

As parents we need to think about the current state of employment, and what skills have helped successful people of all ability levels on the spectrum get and keep jobs or clients. We also need to consider our children's social skills, communication abilities, interdependent skills, and organizational needs.

Let's be frank: having a child with a disability takes a big toll on your pocketbook. Many individuals will need twenty-four-hour supports. Our adults with autism need to work, earn some money, and contribute to society. Yet this is not easy. In actuality, the disabled population is only a tiny percentage of the population of people looking for jobs.

We need to be doing a better job preparing our teens and young adults for employment during their high school and college years. But just as importantly, we need to be educating workplaces, job coaches, corporations, and business leaders about the benefits of hiring a person on the spectrum. We need to convince the Department of Vocational Rehabilitation that many on the spectrum have useful skills and can be successful performing a variety of jobs.

Thanks to the dire state of the economy, many of us are becoming more involved in our communities. We are developing relationships that may help our adult children, and they are learning from us about the importance of interdependence and how to relate to other people. While getting to know more about your community, you can start thinking about what market gaps exist and how you can turn them into work opportunities with the help of your connections. There are many exciting employment programs being developed right now for adults on the spectrum at large corporations and small businesses.

In this chapter, we will discuss our journey so far, the different work structures, how to prepare your son or daughter for employment, and what businesses are doing to successfully hire people on the spectrum. By planning and being proactive, we can find a way for our adult children to hold a job or earn money through self-employment.

THE STATISTICS

The statistics are not surprising, but they're important to understanding how serious the unemployment situation is for those on the spectrum.

According to the organization Easter Seals, only 22 percent of individuals with autism over the age of sixteen are engaged in paid employment, compared with 75 percent of nonautistic individuals as reported by their parents. Twelve percent of nonautistic individuals had not looked for work, compared with 59 percent of individuals with autism. As well, 66 percent of parents of nonautistic children believed that in the future they will be able to work for pay if they want or need to, compared to 16 percent of those on the spectrum.

The US Bureau of Labor Statistics reported in December 2010 that only 21 percent of all adults with disabilities participated in the labor force, compared with 69 percent of the nondisabled population (December 2010 Current Population Survey).

According to the 2002 report by the President's Commission on Excellence in Special Education, 70 percent of disabled working-age adults were unemployed, and these figures were considered to be true for the twelve years preceding. This high rate is why, when the Individuals with Disabilities in Education Act (IDEA) was reauthorized in 2004, the Individual Transition Plan section was strengthened in order to ensure that the school districts were showing more positive outcomes with the transition planning services provided during the high school and transition program years.

About 1 million people in the United States are diagnosed with an Autism Spectrum Disorder, and 80 percent of those identified are younger than twenty-two years old, according to the Organization for Autism Research (OAR). This means that we will have many more adults with autism in a few years. Thus the importance of finding solutions to the high unemployment rate.

STATE AND FEDERAL EMPLOYMENT AGENCIES

Research by Scott Standifer, Ph.D., of the Disability and Policy Studies department at the University of Missouri shows that many of the current practices in training individuals on the spectrum have been ineffective. Many traditional vocational rehabilitation (VR) practices are distressing to the adult with autism. One state Voc Rehab agency reported that of eligible clients with an ASD whom counselors had sent for vocational evaluation, more than 90 percent withdrew from VR services before finishing the evaluation. In addition, there are major concerns with the job coaches and their knowledge of autism, which in turn affects job training. Another concern is the lack of practical suggestions provided on how to capture these job seekers' potential, taking into consideration the remarkable diversity of people with ASD.

In order to fill the existing gap of information available to state employment agencies, Standifer authored *Adult Autism and Employment: A Guide for Vocational Rehabilitation Professionals* in 2009. It is available for free online and is a great resource. Parents and young adults may want to refer to this guide and share it with their local employment offices if they need more autism-specific information.

James Emmett is a national leader in development of employment services for individuals with disabilities and

contributed greatly to Standifer's employment guide. Emmett states that the Department of Vocational Rehabilitation
(DVR), or the Department of Rehabilitation (DOR)—different states may have different names—is a system that was
originally built for the physically disabled, usually those with
visual and auditory challenges. They were not equipped for
working with people with autism or with the learning disabled. This explains why state agencies do not have a good
track record helping adults with autism become employable
or find jobs. According to Emmett, this is improving, as some
states are actively looking to train their employees in this area.

THE FRUSTRATIONS OF TRYING TO GET HELP: WHY THE UNEMPLOYMENT RATE IS SO HIGH

In discussion with Emmett, I shared Jeremy's experience with
our local employment agency, described below. Emmett said
that although some areas of the country fare better than others, he was not surprised by what I recounted. It's a given that
dealings with bureaucratic systems are complicated and lengthy.
However, consider the person with AS with communication
and social challenges attempting to navigate these systems.
Parents used to navigating mandated special education services
need to prepare for the challenges of negotiating for adult services, and must prepare their adult child to do so as well. For
this reason, we share our experience.

In California, Workability is a state-funded program that
provides pre-employment skill and worksite training. In some
school districts, Workability is administered by the DOR. In
others, it is administered by the school district, requiring students to register for DOR services separately. Such was the case
for Jeremy, who had to apply for DOR services without the
help of the school district. The process turned out to be frus-
trating. After filling out a form online, we had to wait a few

months before meeting with Jeremy's assigned counselor. After an initial two-hour meeting with the counselor, we were told we had been assigned to the wrong office and were directed to start over. After a few more phone calls and discussion with an area manager, it was finally straightened out.

A few months later we received a summons from DOR to make an appointment for Jeremy to be seen by a psychologist with no information as to what the meeting was for. When we arrived for the appointment, we were told it was to see whether Jeremy was "college material." Before performing an assessment, the psychologist noted that Jeremy had graduated from high school with a high GPA, and that he had already attended a class at the local community college and received an A. He wondered why we were sent over. Then Jeremy was requested to take part in an academic assessment for which he had no prior warning and did not have the communication devices with him that he uses for test taking at college.

Three months later, Jeremy's case manager and the supervisor told us that the next step was another assessment for Jeremy to evaluate his work skills. The assessment would take place at a well-known, sheltered workshop for people with developmental disabilities. I asked for clarification about what the assessment was for, and what he would be required to do; they did not know but said they would find out. Two months later, when the supervisor called to set up the appointment, I asked her again, and she said she did not know, but that it was the next step if Jeremy wanted any help from the DOR. Then the supervisor proceeded to tell me that Jeremy's idea of trying to make money online using his writing skills was unrealistic. However, when I tried to draw her into discussion about Jeremy's plan, it was apparent that her knowledge of earning income with the use of the Internet was very limited.

In other words, be prepared to face numerous challenges and bureaucratic roadblocks as well as individuals who are not sensitive to your adult child's needs. Understand that there are many communication challenges that will make it difficult for a person on the spectrum to navigate on their own. The people charged with assisting your adult child may not be progressive or technologically knowledgeable.

From discussions with parents and educators around the country at conferences where I present, I know that Jeremy's experience is not an isolated case. As well, when asked about what job their adult child has found through DOR, in about 90 percent of the cases the adult is bagging groceries and stocking shelves at a supermarket, or sweeping the floor and wiping the tables at a restaurant. The sad part is, many of these workers are individuals with AS or high-functioning autism who graduated from high school.

It is important that parents and their adult children realize that they are capable of more, but that it is the system that is failing them. This is why it is important for parents and educators to get involved early in the child's life to discover and build on strengths and passions. Finding mentors who can help translate those strengths into a career or marketable skills is extremely helpful. It is never too late, but the problem is that the older they get, if they have suffered many disappointments and have low self-esteem, it may be hard to get them enthusiastic to try again.

If your child is able, though, it is important to try to find a way through family and community connections to make your adult child feel worthwhile and employable. Do not accept the failings of the system to mean that your adult child is unemployable except in certain menial jobs. When it comes to providing employment opportunities for those with developmental disabilities, state employment agencies often focus on the "4F jobs": food, filth, filing, and flowers. Granted, as neurotypical students, we may have started in those jobs to earn money, but we didn't all expect as grownups to continue sweeping floors, wiping tables, and bagging groceries. I'm not knocking those who enjoy that kind of work. But there should be a lot more variety in employment for those on the spectrum, as there are a lot more talents people have, and there are so many technological advances to help us now.

I feel confident that with perseverance, Jeremy will be able to find his niche, but we will have to do it with the help of our community and connections.

JEREMY:

My mom took me to the Department of Rehabilitation. I must say that they are frankly out-of-date. I'm not an expert on employment, but I really think that if you are going to be advising disabled people on how to make money in 2011 you should be familiar with technological devices like the iPad. And you should be able to get a copy of a report to the person you are helping in less than three months.

I know my mom will have to be my employment counselor because frankly the Department of Rehabilitation has no clue what to do for me. I think basically that my mom would do a better job. I just feel grateful that my mom never gives up.

WHAT OTHERS ON THE SPECTRUM HAVE TO SAY

For those who make it through the process of getting a job, there are other hurdles. John is a personable young man with high-functioning autism who is attending college and working part-time at a movie theater. John worked part-time at three different supermarkets before his current position and was fired from each of them.

At his first job at a supermarket, John would have questions about the placement of items when stocking shelves. Other workers would get irritated when he disrupted their work to ask questions. Eventually he was fired. At the second store, one worker, Greg, would take the time to explain where things were, but when he quit his job at the store for another opportunity,

John had no one left to explain things to him, and he was fired for not being able to complete his job. At this point, his mother sought out the services of job coaches (one-on-one training on a job site) through DOR. John was found a job in a third store. Over a three-year period and with six different coaches, John was provided a few hours of job coaching a week by job coaches who had no particular knowledge about successful strategies for coaching a person with autism. It appeared to John as if the job coaches helped him keep his job by convincing the store manager to keep him on, yet gave no input to the store supervisors or John on strategies to help the job placement be a successful one.

John's challenges in his job were mainly due to his social and communication skills. For example, at the last supermarket, he was told to put away all the carts in the parking lot before taking a break. John took this very literally. As customers were constantly exiting the store and leaving shopping carts, John would not take a break. Then he would get overwhelmed and anxious. One day in this state he was trying to quickly cross the parking lot, and he scratched a Mercedes that was driving by. Another time, he got into an argument with a customer when he told him to "have a nice day" and the customer didn't respond.

After he got fired, John applied for a job at a local movie theater. He and his family decided not to involve the job coaches. So far he is happily employed, and his supervisor and the other employees seem to think he is a cool coworker.

Unfortunately, John's experiences are not uncommon. The challenges these young people face with social skills and communication, coupled with the lack of awareness on the part of supervisors, make for a difficult situation for employers and employees alike. John's experience also illustrates the importance of using job coaches who are familiar with on-the-job strategies that are effective for people with autism. Later in this chapter we will be discussing some of them.

AUTISM ADVOCACY ORGANIZATIONS
AND HOW THEY ARE HELPING

Autism advocacy organizations may have points of disagreement, but there is one area in which all agree: there needs to be more employment opportunity for adults on the spectrum. Many of them are actively working on changing the status quo, and their websites are listed in the resources section so that the reader can keep up with any developments.

In 2009, a national consortium called Advancing Futures for Adults with Autism (AFAA) was formed to facilitate the development of a national agenda on issues affecting adults with autism. Many autism advocacy organizations were involved, and input was taken for this national agenda from many families and advocates all around the country in town hall meetings. This agenda was provided to federal policy makers in July 2010 and its adoption urged.

In the area of employment, AFAA identified many concerns in the autism community, and suggestions on what needs to happen were made. These are:

- **There is a disconnect from the transition years at school to adult life.** Autism educators need to recognize the need to develop employment skills in individuals with autism during the transition years at high school to college and beyond. There needs to be a continuum of support to help individuals with ASD, their families, professionals, and employers.
- **We need to change the mainstream perception of adults with autism.** There needs to be a "presumption of employability," which currently does not exist. As well, the bar needs to be raised when thinking of employment opportunities, and employers need awareness and training. One way would be to make autism a diversity issue, as

employers understand and relate to the importance of diversity matters.

- **Many are underpaid and passed over for promotions.** There needs to be equitable compensation and career opportunities that are mutually beneficial for employers and workers. As well, workers must continue to maintain public assistance benefits—including transportation—even if they have jobs. There is a current disincentive to work, with low wages and loss of assistance benefits for anyone who takes a low-level job.
- **Continual social skills training and lifelong support.** Technically savvy and motivated people are needed to coach, teach, and support those preparing for employment. Without comprehensive help, people on the spectrum will continue to have low expectations for their career opportunities, and so will any potential employers.

EMPLOYERS MAKING A DIFFERENCE

Here are examples of corporations that are committed to hiring people on the spectrum, and that are doing so successfully. They are successful because they are aware of the needs of employees with autism. Some of the effective strategies they use are described later in this chapter.

- **Walgreens** (Walgreensoutreach.com) sets the standards for corporations employing people on the autism spectrum and is successful beyond what was expected. Someone high up in the company has a young adult son with autism, so he got this project going.
- **Home Depot** (homedepot.com): Kenneth Langone, cofounder of the Home Depot, has been instrumental in providing jobs to many individuals with developmental disabilities including autism, through Ken's Krew. Ken's Krew is a nonprofit corporation that provides vocational training and job placement services to young adults with

intellectual and learning disabilities who are transitioning into the workforce. In fact, when the Home Depot
Foundation announced in 2008 a three-year, $1 million
grant to support expansion of the Ken's Krew program
(see below), Langone matched this $1 million grant.

- **Best Buy** (www.bestbuy.com): Disability outreach initiatives are intended to make Best Buy one of the top
  employers/retailers of choice for people interested in the
  disability community.
- **TIAA-CREF** (tcasset.org/innovation-stories/fruits-empl
  oyment-program): Heather Davis, Senior Managing Director and parent of a child on the spectrum, was part of a
  team that proposed the company diversify its investments
  by purchasing farms. TIAA employed autistic individuals for the apple harvest during picking season at Badger
  Mountain, and "Fruits of Employment" was born. This
  strategy delivered cost efficiencies because of the depend-
  ibility and low attrition rate of employees on the spectrum.

PARENTS ACTIVELY MAKING A DIFFERENCE

You don't have to be a major corporation to create change.
There are many more stories of parents actively creating jobs
for one or more people with autism. These are just a few to
inspire you.

- **Specialisterne** (The Specialists), at http://specialisterne
  .com/, is a Danish for-profit social enterprise business
  that has become a worldwide model. It provides software
  testing services using the strengths of adults on the spectrum as a competitive advantage in the business market.
  Specialisterne was started in 2004 by Thorkil Sonne,
  whose son was given a diagnosis of infantile autism, normal intelligence, at age three.
- **Ken's Krew** was founded in 1997 by two sets of parents
  who hoped their children would have fulfilling jobs when

they became adults. Since then they have successfully placed two hundred young adults at seventy-five Home Depot and fifteen CVS Caremark stores as well as other companies.

- **Aspiritech** is a nonprofit based in Highland Park, Illinois, that was inspired by Specialisterne and founded in 2007 by Brenda and Moshe Weitzberg. It has ten employees on the spectrum, others training in software testing, and five client companies.
- **Artistas Café**: "Change Lives One Bean at a Time." Founded by a parent, they opened the first café at Mercedes Benz of Tampa, which has been a success for the dealership as well as the café. All the employees have autism, and there are plans to open more of these.
- **America's Best Train and Hobby Shoppe:** This is a family-run store whose owners have a son with autism. They have hired a young man with autism, and implemented strategies for his employment to be a success. Even small businesses, with the right supports, can successfully provide work for someone on the spectrum.
- **Real People Real Jobs: Stories from the Front Line** (www .realworkstories.org): This website by the Institute for Community Inclusion at the University of Massachusetts Boston has many examples of people working in different job structures such as traditional employment, customized employment, and self-employment (explained in this chapter).

GETTING A JOB OR CLIENT

The reality is that getting and keeping a job or clients is all about relationships and executive functions (planning and organizing), areas that are challenging for most young adults on the spectrum. To get a job, a person needs to know how to convince someone to hire them. Once they are hired, they need to know about the interdependent relationships at work: who the boss is and what he wants from you; how and when to address the supervisor; how to address a customer; how to communicate to their colleagues; whom to approach for help. If they know and understand those rules, and they can plan and stay organized enough to get their work done, they stand a good chance of keeping their job.

Basics to Work on Before They Are Old Enough to Work

Autism is a spectrum, and the talents, strengths, and support needs are different. However, keep in mind that being ready to work doesn't happen overnight for any of us. It's a process that starts when we are young. Here are some general tips:

1. **Raise your child to have high self-esteem: believe in your child.** Henry Ford once said, "If you think you can or can't, you're right." It is important to raise all children to believe they have positive attributes and qualities, and this is done by focusing on the positive, not the negatives. As parents of children with IEPs we learn to focus on the child's deficits, and this is not conducive to building one's confidence. Wherever possible, notice your child's strengths, reinforce them, praise him for them. It is the strengths that will help him as an adult, not the areas that he has troubles with.

2. **Make sure your young adult has advocacy skills.** At any job, no matter his ability level, your adult child will need to be able to advocate for himself with whatever form of communication he uses. If your child is on the more able end of the spectrum and you do not have conservatorship for him, he will be the one making decisions for himself. Huge systems such as Vocational Rehabilitation are mind-boggling and difficult for anyone to navigate, let alone a person who has communication and

social difficulties. On the job, he will need to be able to speak up for himself to have his needs met.

3. **Teach your child manners and as much as possible the ways of the neurotypical world.** Everyone must learn to greet people, say thank you, keep and smell clean, not grab others' belongings or touch certain body parts in public. Potential employers will forgive quirkiness if a potential hire is talented, but some bad manners are nonnegotiable the higher up the employee chain a person strives to be.

4. **Ensure that your adult child can "sell" his attributes and skill set.** Arm your child with a list of qualities they have: "I am always on time and never sick"; "I am honest and truthful"; "I am passionate about having all objects neatly stacked on shelves facing the right way." A person must have a way of selling his skill. A graphic designer or a writer can produce samples of their work. People who do not have samples to show will need a description of how their strengths will match the job.

5. **Provide opportunities for your teen to experience task completion, the idea of responsibility, and the pleasure of doing something for someone.** Try to figure out a way for your child to gain experience in work and responsibility. Does the pet store need dog walkers? Does the neighbor need help with certain chores? Giving your child chores around the house is a good way to teach responsibility. One summer Jeremy and a support person delivered Meals on Wheels to seniors in their homes. Both Jeremy and the seniors were happy to see each other. Jeremy had to learn not to touch the decorations on their front doors—that was a positive by-product.

6. **Increase your child's stamina.** Often our young people on the spectrum do not get enough exercise, as they are not usually involved in sports. It's important to put reg-

ular exercise into their schedule. This is important for health reasons but also to develop the stamina needed to work for an extended period of time without becoming tired.

Things for Parents to Consider

The foundation for success in helping your adult child find employment or earn a living is really the attitude that you take as you approach the process. Here are some guidelines to consider:

- **Shift the focus from deficits to strengths.** For parents, the shift from school to work will require a different mind-set. Instead of focusing on the deficits, as is often done in the special education setting, parents will need to focus on the strengths of their adult child in order to get them certain job experiences or to get them into the programs that exist.
- **Accept that you have to be involved.** There is a certain peace that comes when after repeated attempts you face the fact that if you want something to happen, you will have to put it together.
- **Understand the mind-set of the systems in place.** Supported employment can be funded through vocational rehabilitation agencies or state Departments of Developmental Disabilities. However, according to the Organization for Autism Research, families will have to advocate strongly for the idea that supported employment, by definition and statute, is intended for people with severe disabilities (they usually use it for more able individuals, i.e., nonautistic people). Parents will also have to convince the government aid agency that individuals with ASD can work if given the proper support, training, and attention to job-match characteristics.

- **Think like an entrepreneur.** You may have never wanted to have your own small business, but you will need to think like an entrepreneur to manage all that it entails to successfully help your adult child get to the point where he has a job or is earning money. If your child has an obsession or special interest, try to find out how he or she could earn money from it.
- **Network: It takes a village—relationships are key.** It is clear that relationships are the key ingredient to your adult child's obtaining work. It is your contacts who are going to help your child find work or a volunteer position or an internship. Your son or daughter must also learn relationship skills to the best of their abilities.

Embracing Difference

There is a common thread in all the success stories of those on the spectrum who are employed, and it is this: wherever they worked they were accepted for who they were. It needs to start with parents recognizing and embracing the positive aspects of the differences their adult child has. These differences may help the person get hired. If a parent does not accept the differences, how can the adult child or a prospective employer be convinced of the value of that person's ability?

Specialisterne, the Danish for-profit social enterprise business that provides software testing services, is using those differences—including the ability of the consultants to stay focused beyond the point when most minds go numb—as a competitive advantage. One client who hired Specialisterne workers to do data entry found that they were five to ten times more precise than other contractors. As a result of being so focused, Aspies make far fewer mistakes. The success of Specialisterne—whose customers include LEGO, Microsoft, and Oracle—is due to its employees on the spectrum, who are paid competitive wages.

Embracing differences also means being understanding of a person's difficulties. Karla, a young woman with Asperger's Syndrome, quit a job because one of her supervisors did not tolerate her difficulties processing many things going on at once. Although the boss and her other supervisor appreciated that she was fully committed, helpful, and diligent, this other supervisor often accused her of being difficult and not listening to her. The supervisor would yell instead of calmly talking to her, leading her to become anxious and fearful. Karla feels that she could have been successful at this job provided that the accommodation was in place that she not be interrupted frequently during tasks.

FINDING A JOB: WHERE TO START

Readers who are familiar with Temple Grandin's life story will remember that she got her first jobs based on her talent and her passion, not her social skills. Although Temple's social skills are good now, they were developed over many years on the job.

Passionate interests (or obsessions, as many professionals label them) can be a lifeline for adults on the spectrum when it comes to employment, if they have mentors who can show them how to earn money from their interest. Temple Grandin often speaks about the importance of mentors in her life. There was her science teacher in high school who encouraged her to pursue science, and her aunt who allowed her to spend time on her farm with the animals. Her first few bosses recognized her talents and gave her advice in other areas that she needed to be successful.

Finding mentors when younger can help develop some of your child's interests into marketable skills. The mentor can help practice social skills needed for interviews and on the job. Often having "social skills" lessons is a good way to learn the basics, but being part of a group with a shared interest can help the person build social skills. Using contacts and community connections is a good way to find mentors.

For those on the more impacted end of the spectrum, use person-centered planning methods described in Chapter 2, such as PATH, to figure out from different people what they see as your adult child's strengths. There are ways of getting ideas by observing people in different environments, with different people doing different activities that help discover the strengths of the individual as well as what they like and what motivates them, which can lead to brainstorming for work possibilities.

Finding the Right Job Structure: Know Thyself

Social demands, sensory issues, and anxiety contribute to the overwhelm that many with autism feel at work. Aspies have a great ability to immerse themselves in work on the job, but the workplace needs to be the right fit.

Michael J. Carley, the executive director of the Global and Regional Asperger Syndrome Partnership, says that the most important key to a successful match is to know yourself thoroughly. This means knowing what you like but also having a good grasp of your personal work style and how that relates to the different jobs out there. The possibility of jobs range from from the arts and university fields (most permissible) to the military (most rigid). Different jobs allow different levels of diversity in physical, vocal, or cerebral expressions. For many on the spectrum who have sensory and emotional overwhelm challenges, it is really important to consider whether they are able to work part-time or full-time. For example, I know a young man who loved his job at a hotel but found that he could tolerate only two days of work straight, and needed one day off to recuperate from the sensory assault to his system. Another could not work in a school environment because there were no break times in which he could decompress from the noise of all the students.

Besides part-time and full-time competitive employment and seasonal work, there is supported employment, which may include a job coach and entrepreneurial supports for those interested in a self-employment model. There are also sheltered workshops, which are restrictive environments where people work for less than minimum wage.

Customized Employment/Self-Employment

Another option that is becoming more and more popular is customized employment, in which the needs of both the employer and the employee are met, based on individualized determination of the strengths and needs of the person with the disability, but also designed to meet the needs of the employer.

One kind of customized employment is job carving, where certain duties from one or more existing jobs are selected and then combined into a new position. This is a way of creating jobs that fit a person's ideal conditions of employment, thus creating a better match for the person and the employer. Job carving can be beneficial for someone who is really good at and enjoys one aspect of a job, but has difficulty with others. The employer benefits from having a focused worker for the areas the person excels in. These jobs can be part-time as well, which better suits some people. As this type of employment is fairly new, it may be up to the parent, the mentor, or the individual to suggest, find, and create the position.

Self-employment or microenterprise is another kind of customized employment in which the passions and talents of the person looking for work are used to earn money by producing a product or providing a service. For those on the more able end of the spectrum, it can mean a traditional full-time or part-time consultancy business in their area of expertise. For those on the more impacted end of the spectrum, the microenterprise can be as big or as little as the person wishes. With the Internet there are great opportunities for finding potential customers.

For this to be successful, a business plan needs to be created, as it is important to know if there is a market for the product or service, and then there needs to be a marketing plan, because that is how possible clients will know about the product or service. Another important consideration is to make sure that all the legal aspects of having a small business are followed.

For self-employment to work, there needs to be a "business support team" of advisors so that if there are questions about bookkeeping, taxes, and so on, there are people who can help. Realize that if your adult child is receiving Supplementary Security Income (SSI), you have to know what the rules and regulations are in terms of earning money and how that affects his eligibility for SSI and other benefits such as Medicare. For any self-employment idea to succeed, however, it has to start with a passion or talent a person has and is interested in pursuing. The discovery of how the person can take a passion and turn it into a moneymaker is an important step. Dusty's Puppets is a well-known example of self-employment based on a passion. Dusty Dutton is a talented and experienced entertainer who has Down syndrome and has always loved storytelling. Now she uses her unique sense of humor to bring hand puppets to life and provides entertainment to children's parties and farmers' markets (http://www.dustyspuppets.com/). There are more links to examples in the resource section. For a basic workbook about self-employment, see *A Self-Employment Guide for Beginners* on AutismCollege.com. Sometimes while going through the process of self-discovery and analyzing the need for the service or product by speaking to community members, an opportunity for traditional employment emerges.

It's important to take into consideration the costs of doing business. If a person needs a one-to-one support person to be successful at doing the work and those hours are not provided by an outside agency, then they are considered a cost of doing business and must be taken into account in the business plan. Think of it this way: if your adult child needs a one-to-one staff person anyway, what better way to spend their time than earning money and at least covering their costs?

There are some work incentives such as Plan to Achieve Self Support (PASS) available through SSI that can be used for needed self-employment equipment (e.g., a delivery truck, computer) if the person is eligible and the project is approved. For more information go to http://www.ssa.gov/disability research/wi/pass.htm.

ADULTS WITH ASPERGER'S SYNDROME: TO DISCLOSE, OR NOT

Many individuals with Asperger's have differing opinions on whether to disclose their diagnosis. Stephen Shore, author of *Ask and Tell*, says that the need for disclosure is directly related to whether all your needs are met in a certain environment. If an adult has no special on-the-job requirements and can communicate sufficiently with colleagues and his or her superiors, then perhaps no disclosure is necessary. Some people with AS decide not to disclose and then handle needs on the job without using their diagnosis. A person may have extreme sensitivity to lights, and may mention that as a workplace concern and ask for different lighting or the permission to wear sunglasses indoors.

However, if a person does not disclose a disability during the hiring process, then he has no legal standing to ask for accommodations under the Americans with Disabilities Act (ADA). ADA protects only employees who have disclosed their disability during the hiring process. Because of the nature of Asperger's Syndrome and the fact that they are usually in an environment with no supports, whether to disclose is an important decision.

Disclosing during the hiring process that you have Asperger's Syndrome can also help ensure that you accept a job at a place that is accepting of differences. Brenda, who has AS, disclosed her diagnosis during the interview for a job as an assistant sports coach at a summer camp. She also disclosed that she had never had a paid summer job as she was afraid of working with other people. Brenda was hired and her employer was very supportive, which helped ease her anxieties and boost her confidence. As an assistant coach, Brenda did a lot of administrative work: keeping a chart of job applicants and résumés submitted, and calling them back using a script for interviews. Brenda also conducted job interviews, sticking to a script of questions, which she thoroughly enjoyed.

MAKING IT THROUGH THE INTERVIEW: HIGHLIGHT SKILLS

The first challenge with any job, no matter the ability level, is making it through the interview process or assessment. Plan on practicing the interview with your child. Role-playing is a good way to lessen anxiety and to practice the expected manners and greetings during an interview. Some employers who have a history of hiring people on the spectrum are familiar with the difficulty that interviewing poses. The Walgreens Distribution Center in Connecticut hires people with autism, and they are aware that some job candidates on the spectrum struggle with the way the interview questions are worded. Therefore, Walgreens has developed a modified script to use during the interview process that eliminates abstract language.

You might feel that your child's social and communication skills are not strong enough to convince someone to give him a job. This is where we all need to think more like marketing executives: we can learn to highlight the positive attributes and downplay the negatives without promising what we can't deliver. After years of special education services, many on the spectrum (as well as parents) are used to focusing on what a person *can't* do, as opposed to focusing on what they *can* do. When it comes to your child, you may not be able to guarantee performance, but you can still point out all the reasons why someone should be given a chance.

Temple Grandin, in her book *Developing Talents*, discusses the importance of creating a portfolio showcasing the talents of a person. This works well for those like Grandin who can show something they've made or drawn. They can also bring in a DVD with images of projects completed to leave with the prospective employer.

The top two skills employers look for, as identified by the Bureau of Labor Statistics (Job Outlook 2003), are honesty and integrity, and a strong work ethic. These are positive traits to highlight. The other top ten skills employers look for include analytical skills; computer skills; teamwork; time management and organizational skills; communication skills; flexibility; interpersonal skills; motivation; and initiative.

Granted, the adult you are thinking of may not have all or many of these, but practically all on the spectrum (provided they are not dual diagnosed with a mental illness) are honest to a fault and have a strong work ethic. And those are the two top skills employers look for—they will show up, and they won't steal. Many of the other attributes can be taught for some, or else some supports can be added. If teamwork is difficult because of social challenges, one person on the team can be delegated as the "go to" person who will be the point of contact for the individual on the spectrum.

Create a résumé highlighting the positive aspects of the person that match any of the top skills ("near-perfect school attendance," "organizes his space and keeps it neat," etc.). Remember to highlight your child's passions. One of my husband's past bosses loves trains and actually owns a small train shop: someone listing trains and why they are interested in them would have been the starting point of any interview.

Those who are on the more impacted end of the spectrum will be accompanied to any interview. Having a résumé that they can hand over and a DVD showing the person actively engaging in some activity demonstrates some of his strengths and interests. Especially if someone easily gets nervous and overwhelmed, a video of what a person is like when they are comfortable in their environment is a good thing to leave behind after an interview. For those who are nonverbal, information that the job seeker wishes to share or questions she wants to ask can already be preprogrammed into her assistive technology device. As well, if a prospective employee has some difficulties, a prepared list of strategies and supports that have worked in the past or would be worth trying could be available.

ASSESSMENTS

This is an integral step to any possible placement in an area of employment that may need supports. Effective assessment includes assessment of the individual but also an analysis of the actual job and the skills needed. This includes:

- A detailed job analysis, similar to a task analysis, where the parts of a job are broken down into smaller steps
- The motor skills that define the job
- The social skills that enable the person to fit into the workplace
- The self-management skills that help the person be autonomous and adaptable
- The academic skills that the person needs to be successful

The employees on the spectrum whom Ken's Krew has placed are typically those with Asperger's Syndrome. Ken's Krew believes that a successful placement depends on a good match between the needs of the store and the abilities of the adult. Skills that are necessary to a successful placement include self-regulation, self-advocacy, good hygiene skills, time-management skills, stamina, volunteer experience, and experience doing chores at home.

Ken's Krew has developed a five-step selection process to placing potential trainees: application, interview, observation, store assessment, and parent interview. This process includes an assessment of the store environment by the person with autism so that they can assess whether they can handle the sensory environment.

The first step is a probation period for the employee and the employer to sample each other. The new employee is assigned a job coach for approximately twelve weeks. During that time, the job coach works hard to put natural supports in place so that the employee does not stay dependent on the coach, and then when the coach is no longer there, the employee has a trusted person or two he can call on.

FORMING RELATIONSHIPS ON THE JOB

You might wonder how your child will feel comfortable in social situations given that individuals on the spectrum often lack natural social affability. They may be happy to see you, but you might not know it by looking at them—they may not greet you with a smile. Employers (and customers) find it hard to connect with someone who does not show interest in the typical social niceties. Then there are the different types of relationships in the workplace.

Success on the Job: Knowing Who Does What

Besides self-awareness, those with autism who have been successful at getting and keeping jobs understand the social relationships at work and learn about the styles of communication. The following practical tips are applicable no matter the job or ability level:

- **Know who the boss is, and what the boss wants.** The new employee must remember what he was hired to do, and do it. He should never threaten his boss's interests or authority. It is important that he remember that he was hired because he can help his boss with work that he does not want to spend effort on or that he cannot do.
- **Know the hierarchy and appropriate forms of communication.** It is important to understand the corporate structure, and what position people hold in this hierarchy. Then,

understanding the different types of appropriate communication to have with the people in different positions
(colleagues, the boss, the CEO, the assistant) is important.
Drawing a visual representation of the different levels of
the hierarchy can be helpful.

- **Have a mentor or trusted peer at work to turn to.** Many
report that a mentor at work was crucial to their success
on the job. A trusted buddy as a social navigator can help
a person respond appropriately in social situations at
work. For those on the more impacted end of the spectrum, a peer buddy can be extremely helpful when the
person needs guidance on the job, or to feel more welcome in a work situation.

- **Use visual aids if needed or a notebook to keep track of
rules and information.** Some adults do well with visual
reminders of sequences and tasks. Still others may write
their own reminders and rules of behaviors in a notebook.
Having a notebook a person can refer to or add to when
necessary is comforting in times of overwhelm.

Relationships with Coworkers

Research indicates that in times of economic turmoil, it is the
person who has a good relationship with the boss and coworkers who keeps the job, while those with poor relationship skills
are let go. However, Ashley Stanford, the CEO of a successful
computer company based in Silicon Valley in California, believes that the "failure to create peer relationships" that is considered an impairment in diagnostic criteria can actually be a
benefit if properly positioned in the workplace. An employee
who does not create peer relationships can be a focused, proj-
ect-driven employee undistracted by others and undeterred by
potentially emotionally volatile problems. This employee usually tends to be more productive than those who spend time
hanging out at the water cooler.

Rudy Simone, who has Asperger's Syndrome, says that employees with AS find the work social environment difficult because they go to work to work, not to socialize. According to Simone, many adults with AS say that their job failures were due to their inability to socialize on the job. A prior understanding of the unspoken job requirements and an explanation of the hidden curriculum at work would most likely have been helpful to them. In academic or cerebral environments, or jobs with like-minded people with shared interests, the lack of social skills is less noticeable.

The friendship skills that are so important in the younger years tend to become less important in full-time employment. CEOs prefer to have colleagues who get along rather than have close-knit friendships, which can be detrimental to a team and directly affect a company's bottom line. For example, if there is a team of nine people, some may be closer friends, which can create jealousies and which can amount to family-like squabbles. As well, it is much more difficult to tell management if a friend rather than just a colleague is doing something dishonest. As well, office romances may occur when people are too close.

In regard to relationship development and on-the-job communication, it is not just the lack of participating in social niceties and understanding the games people play that can be challenging. Nonverbal behavior can be daunting as well—both trying to decode the signals of others as well as trying to learn how to send signals. For example, eye contact can be difficult for a person on the spectrum, and if a person does not give any contact, it is considered rude. But if a person stares in someone's eyes for too long, or stares at another part of someone's body, it can be considered rude as well.

The Asperger Syndrome Employment Workbook, by Roger N. Meyer (who has AS), has great worksheets in the back to help adults with autism analyze past work experiences, on-the-job levels of social skill understanding, and possible tools and strategies to use to be successful in the work environment.

Relationship with the Manager

The most important work relationship that exists at work is the one between the employee and his supervisor. The most important aspect of any employee-boss relationship is respect: respect that the employee with AS has for himself, and respect for his boss. Respect for himself means that if he is really uncomfortable with socializing at lunchtime, he should say, "Thanks, but I'm busy." If the employee with AS puts himself in too many uncomfortable positions, he may experience overload and not be able to adequately get his job done. Treating the boss in a respectful manner and producing great work on time are two goals every person (on and off the spectrum) should aspire to.

Managers need to learn some communications strategies as well. Temple Grandin suggests that the key to successfully communicating with an Aspie is to be specific. For example, don't tell an Aspie that the lunchroom is open from eleven to one, or he may think that means he can have a two-hour lunch. The supervisor needs to clearly state that lunch is a forty-five-minute time slot to be taken anywhere between eleven and one.

In describing behaviors, such as "don't be rude to customers," explain that they must say hello to each customer they pass, that they are not to follow potential customers around the store, or whatever the desired outcome is.

SKILLS, ACCOMMODATIONS, AND SUPPORTS

What are the main skills that your child needs to function successfully in a work environment, and what accommodations can help them be successful?

Self-Advocacy

An important life skill, as mentioned in earlier chapters, is self-advocacy. Zosia Zaks, an independent vocational rehabilitation counselor on the spectrum, explains that a person does not need to be verbal to advocate for himself. There are simple, low-tech ways of communicating one's needs. A young man she knows carries an index card with a red stripe on one side and a green stripe on the other side. If he does not understand what the boss wants him to do, he shows his boss the red stripe to avoid more agitation and anxiety. When the boss sees the red stripe, she is careful not to overwhelm him further. When he flashes the red stripe, she stops talking, switches to visual instructions, and gives him a few minutes of breathing room. Conversely, when he is comfortable with a set of instructions, or feels ready to proceed with the next activity, he shows his green stripe.

Flexibility

Flexibility is important on the job, yet it can be difficult to teach. Zosia Zaks explains that it is a good idea to build up tolerance for changes to the schedule, or other types of disruptions and interruptions. As well, those on the spectrum need to be able to tolerate suggestions from coworkers and the supervisor. One way to do that is by rehearsing what they would do and/or say. Writing conversation scripts in advance can help. Having a way to respond when asked to do something new would give your adult child the time he needs to switch gears, accept new instructions, prepare himself for a new experience, or cope with his emotions about the change in appropriate ways. Visual aids such as "if/then" flow charts can help with handling change as well. If he is nonverbal, or talking under stress is too difficult, he could utilize communication cards and other visual strategies to get his point across.

Executive Functions, Organization, Task Completion

Organization, scheduling, task completion, and information recall can be difficult for the employee with an autism spectrum disorder. We discuss these executive functions for those with

Asperger's Syndrome, but all jobs, no matter how basic, require some executive functions. The strategies used to provide supports or help in these areas depend on the ability level of the employee and on the job.

Luckily, there are now so many types of organizational strategies available—either on computers, online, on cell phones, or on paper—that a good fit can be found for any person who needs it. The important thing is to be able to analyze job requirements, the strengths of the employee with autism, and the organizational techniques that will support that person's needs so he is able to complete projects on time. Examples of strategies that have been successful include:

- Transitions between tasks, or when something unexpected occurs, can be tricky. Walgreens uses touchscreen computers with large icons and easy-to-read type to give employees reminders of what to do when change happens. As well, they put messages on computer screens, or on and around the employees' workstations.
- Aspiritech helps its ten staff members on the spectrum complete projects by providing any needed accommodations, which may include written routines, posted schedules, calendars, checklists, timers, preparations to cope with change and transitions, and/or electric organizers.
- Two accommodations that Home Depot has put into effect to foster the success of the placement is to commit to a set schedule for the employee on the spectrum and ensure that the employee will never be alone on the floor. During these economically challenging times, this is no small accommodation, and it really shows their commitment to helping employees be successful on the job. However, for a hiring program such as this to be successful, there must be support and buy-in from store management and associates.
- Many on the spectrum report that a mentor at work was crucial to their success on the job. Having a trusted buddy

as a social navigator can help a person respond appropriately in social situations at work. For those on the more impacted end of the spectrum, a mentor can be extremely helpful when the person needs guidance on the job, or to feel more welcome in a work situation.

- Some adults do well with visual reminders of sequences and tasks. Still others may write their own reminders and rules of behavior in a notebook. Having a notebook a person can refer to or add to when necessary is comforting in times of overwhelm.

- Technology can be used to lessen the dependence on others for task completion. Digitally recorded auditory-prompt systems of step-by-step instructions can be played back through headsets. There are different applications using visual and auditory prompts that can be downloaded into phones and other devices for learners at www.iprompts.com. Phones, iPads, and other devices are helping those who require more supervision and prompting to self-manage, and thus become more independent.

- Some people find that having a favorite item to hold helps with transition. Some have been able to transfer this to having a photo of the item as the screensaver on their iPhone or iPad.

Personal Awareness, Sensory Challenges at Work

Brian King, LCSW, has AS and is the father of three boys on the spectrum. As a coach to parents and their children on the spectrum, Brian emphasizes the need for personal awareness. For a person to be successful on the job, he needs to be able to see the "problems of the space," meaning the sensory issues in that environment.

The founders of Aspiritech, being parents themselves of a young adult on the spectrum, understand the need that many have for a quiet work environment. Feeling comfortable and safe is a basic need for everyone at work. Those with sensory challenges may need adjustments to their environment, or on their person. Practical solutions that have worked for others include:

- Those who need sensory input and who benefited from wearing weighted vests at school may find that wearing heavier-than-normal fabrics and adding coins or other heavy objects in the pockets of jackets and pants is helpful.
- For problems with noise, wearing headphones for music or even white-noise programs on the computer can be helpful.
- Having fidgety types of items in a desk drawer or pocket for discreet use when needed can help. Hanging small pictures of a favorite cartoon character or person in the work area can also make a person feel more secure.
- Lowering the lights, if you have your own workspace, or putting a lamp on your desk that knocks out the effects of fluorescent lights can be helpful.

Some of these ideas may not seem all that different from what some people do with their workspace anyway, but it can make all the difference to someone on the spectrum.

JEREMY:

I want to say that I have had small self-employment experiences that have helped me learn about earning money. I learned that if I wanted customers I needed to have a product or service that people wanted to buy. Also I had to have marketing skills and had to bring in enough money to make a profit.

I do not understand the reason for having a boring job unless you are getting well paid. I think it is just unrealistic to expect people with autism to work hard to learn skills to apply to a job they hate. Hopefully they are enjoying what they are doing. My mom tells me

I am not realistic about hoping that all people will enjoy their work, but I have to believe people must be working hard for something other than money.

I want to realize my dream of giving back to the autism community. Some people tell me that I give people a better idea of what autism is than some professionals. I know there is a lot of misunderstanding about what we can and can't do and what we need to succeed. I often saw my mom explaining to teachers how to work with me. I want to help people understand how to help someone like me communicate and learn.

I wrote my own monthly column in my high school newspaper, "Life As I See It," and I have written articles for a couple of autism magazines. Now I am a staff writer on my community college newspaper. I would like to do more presentations to schools on how to include a person with disabilities and give tips on how to act with differently abled students. I could do talks specifically to autism as well. I think I can be a good example of overcoming challenges and never giving up. I have already given a few presentations, but I was very nervous and it was not always a success.

My fear of presenting comes from the nervousness that I might get overwhelmed by noise and light and that people might try to touch me without asking first. I am working on this and it is getting better. Like for all my other obstacles, I know with planning and practice I can improve. I think if I practice to get over my nervousness, I can get better with presenting.

JEREMY'S TOP TEN HELPFUL TIPS FOR PARENTS ON EMPLOYMENT

1. **Try to find something your son or daughter likes to do.** I understand why work is important, but why would you continue working if you are unhappy?
2. **Invest some time in trying to see if there is work or a market for a talent they have.** If they have a special interest, look to see how they can earn money from it.

3. **Have loving, thoughtful support staff or job coaches.** Make sure they are able to comprehend the ways to help your son or daughter focus, and the way they need help with their movements.

4. **Have them get a job because it helps with socialization.** They can make nice contacts with neurotypicals in this way.

5. **Help them with making money.** Support this by nicely being there for them and telling them that they can succeed.

6. **Teach your child "on-the-job" skills.** I am not an expert on skill-building, but how can they know the skills if they are not taught them or born knowing them?

7. **Teach them real-life skills.** For example, teach them how to stay calm and keep their hands to themselves. It is not appropriate to touch other people's things in the workplace.

8. **Voice to them what they are expected to do.** I like it when I am told what I am expected to do, because I don't always know what I am expected to do in different situations.

9. **Help give them building blocks for being successful.** For example, teach them the importance of finishing what they start.

10. **Don't give up on your child.** My mom was told to give up. We did not. Really, it is important to do anything that is helpful.

RESOURCES

Books:

Adult Autism & Employment: A Guide for Vocational Rehabilitation Professionals, Scott Standifer

Asperger Syndrome Employment Workbook: An Employment Workbook for Adults with Asperger Syndrome, Roger Meyer

Asperger's on the Job: Must-Have Advice for People with Asperger's or High Functioning Autism and Their Employers, Educators, and Advocate, Rudy Simone

Autism and the Transition to Adulthood: Success Beyond the Classroom, Paul Wehman et al.

Autism Life Skills, Chantal Sicile-Kira

A Beginner's Guide to Self-Employment, Chantal Sicile-Kira

Business for Aspies: 42 Best Practices for Using Asperger's Syndrome Traits at Work Successfully, Ashley Stanford

Developing Talents: Careers for Individuals with Asperger Syndrome and High-Functioning Autism, Temple Grandin and Kate Duffy

How to Find Work That Works for People with Asperger's Syndrome, Gail Hawkins

The Job Developer's Handbook: Practical Tactics for Customized Employment, Cary Griffin, David Hammis, and Tammara Geary

Life and Love: Positive Strategies for Autistic Adults, Zosia Zaks

Making Self-Employment Work for People with Disabilities, Cary Griffin and David Hammis

Systematic Instruction of Functional Skills for Students and Adults with Disabilities, Keith Storey

Working Relationships: Creating Career Opportunities for Job Seekers with Disabilities through Employer Partnerships, Richard G. Luecking, Ellen S. Fabian, and George P. Tilson

Nonprofit Autism Organizations with Employment-Related Information:

ASTEP (Asperger Syndrome Training and Employment Partnership), http://asperger-employment.org/

Autism Society of America, http://www.autism-society.org/

Autism Speaks, http://www.autismspeaks.org/

Autistic Global Initiative, http://www.autismwebsite.com/agi/index.html

GRASP (The Global Regional Asperger Syndrome Partnership), http://www.grasp.org/

The National Autism Resource and Information Center, http://autismnow.org/about-us/

Movie:

Temple Grandin, http://www.hbo.com/movies/temple-grandin
/index.html

Websites:

Autism College Library, http://autismcollege.com/library/
Disability Benefits 10: Working with a Disability in California,
www.DB101.org
Jobs 4 Autism, http://www.jobs4autism.com/
JobTIPS, http://www.do2learn.com/JobTIPS/index.html
PASS Plan to Achieve Self-Support, http://www.ssa.gov/disability
research/wi/pass.htm
Real People Real Jobs: Stories from the Front Line—Institute for
Community at University of Massachusetts Boston, http://
realworkstories.org/
US Small Business Administration, www.sba.gov (includes SCORE,
Women's Business Center)

CLOSING COMMENTS

Finding Our Way Together to Create Positive Outcomes

If you treat an individual as if he were what he ought to be and could be, he will become all that he is capable of becoming.

—Johann Wolfgang von Goethe

Looking to the future I see great realizations of my hopes that life will be happy and love-filled.

—Jeremy

We have an ongoing joke at home about what Jeremy's future living situation should look like. While Jeremy has his eye on the HBO show *Entourage*, in which four guy friends share bachelor digs in LA, I have my sights set on HBO's *Big Love*. Having three wives, a three-house suburban home base, an extended family, and strong community ties sounds like a good model for what Jeremy's future should look like. With three wives, Jeremy would have the love and intimacy he craves, and the women would have plenty of respite. This arrangement would also solve the housing problem and our worries about what will happen when his father and I are no longer alive. For now, I keep searching for ways for him to connect and relate with people, to find ways to teach him, and to help him reach his goals of "having the love of a good woman," as he so aptly puts it.

But all kidding aside, I believe that by continuing to strengthen our community ties and by acting like social entrepreneurs, we can create a future for our children that includes a good quality of life. I'm grateful for those in the community who have worked hard to protect the rights of our children and adults. We must continue what has been started to ensure that the futures of our children continue to evolve in a positive direction. In our own way, we can each be a positive force for change.

JEREMY:

I like to think like a good man once told me: you are the product of your parents and the product of your environment, and the reaction you have to both. If you are a hard worker and have great parents and a good school, you will be successful. That is the story of how I came out of darkness.

I just have to tell everyone that getting out of the darkness was not a miracle. It was a team effort of lots of work over a long period of time. The real reason for my success is frankly that my mom got good people to work with me and professionals who believed in me.

Recently I had a dream that this book was a best seller. Mom was in a bookstore and she asked the bookseller where our book was and the person said they could not keep it in stock. People read it and got lots of ideas to make their lives better. They built a society that recognized how we are differently abled.

The adult services in place are not worried about what the adult child really thinks, and they want them to exhibit behaviors that are socially acceptable. They expect the adult child to want to think like neurotypicals. The reality is we need supports to do that. It takes a very strong person to understand what I need to be successful. It takes someone who can free their heart.

Life is not just about work. It is about the nice friends we could have. Making friends is not easy, but I have to say it is not that hard if you find the right people. Hope is the key to our future. You, the parent, need to be positive. It can be very hard at times, but realize that your adult child deserves both understanding and happiness. Humor is helpful because if you can't laugh sometimes, you will bring both sadness and great frustration to your friends and family.

Honor your adult child's future by creating a kick-ass team of supports. Be careful about the adults who are there to support your child. They must be a good match and well trained because your adult child relies on them to feel safe. I know it is hard and I know my mom is tired, but success makes it worthwhile.

I think I have a bright future ahead. I know life will not be easy, but I look forward to doing my best. I hope I will be able to overcome the obstacles I face to live the life of a young man who wishes to help the world be a better place for all people.

BIBLIOGRAPHY

Advancing Futures for Adults with Autism (2010a). "Advancing Futures for Adults with Autism Congressional Report." AFAA, http://www.afaaus .org/site/c.llIYIkNZJuE/b.5063863/k.BE3C/Home.htm.

——— (2009b). "Think Tank Summary Report." AFFA, www.afaa-us.org/atf /cf/ ... 1EB0 ... /Think_Tank_Summary_Report.pdf.

——— (2009c). "About AFAA/Overview." Advancing Futures for Adults with Autism, http://www.afaa-us.org/site/c.llIYIkNZJuE/b.5063941/k.E26 E/Overview.htm.

Allen, K. D., D. P. Wallace, D. J. Greene, S. L. Bowen, and R. V. Burke (2010). "Community-Based Vocational Instruction Using Videotaped Modeling for Young Adults with Autism Spectrum Disorders Performing in Air-Inflated Mascots." *Focus on Autism and Other Developmental Disabilities,* September, 186–92.

Amos, P. (2010). "It's About Relationships: For You, For Your Child." YAP, Inc., http://www.yapinc.org/index.php?fuseAction=searches .dispSearch& searchID=1&pID=1&q=its+about+relationships.

Attwood, T. (2009). "Romantic Relationships for Young Adults with Asperger's Syndrome and High-Functioning Autism." Interactive Autism Network, http://www.iancommunity.org/cs/articles/relationships;jsession id=aIZytspmD8b9WLHeAa.

Baker, J. (2006). *Preparing for Life: The Complete Guide for Transitioning to Adulthood for Those with Autism and Asperger's Syndrome.* Arlington, Texas: Future Horizons.

Beer, J. (2010). "Communicating Across Cultures: High and Low Context." JB Intercultural Consulting, http://www.culture-at-work.com/index .html.

Bellini, S. (2006). *Building Social Relationships: A Systematic Approach to Teaching Social Interaction Skills to Children and Adolescents with Autism Spectrum Disorders and Other Social Difficulties.* Shawnee Mission, Kansas: Autism Asperger Publishing Co.

Bennett, D. (2009). "Thorkil Sonne: Recruit Autistics." *Wired.*

Blacher, J., B. R. Kraemer, and E. J. Howell (in press). "Family Expectations and Transition Experiences for Young Adults with Intellectual Disability: Does Syndrome Matter?" *Advances in Mental Health and Learning Disabilities.*

Boycott, N. (2008). "Creating Programs for Sociosexual Development in Adolescents." Cheri, http://www.cheri.com.au/documents/CreatingProgs forSSDinAdolsCHERISept08.pdf.

Carley, J. M. (2008). *Asperger's from the Inside Out: A Practical and Supportive Guide for Anyone with Asperger's Syndrome.* New York: Penguin.

Cendrowski, S. (2011). "Autism's New Venture Capitalists." *CNN,* http://finance.fortune.cnn.com/2011/06/09/autisms-new-venture-capitalists/.

Crumm, E., and W. Burns (2011). "Finding Solutions: Beyond Brochures." Think College, www.thinkcollege.net.

Danya International Inc. (2006). *Life Journey Through Autism: A Guide for Transition to Adulthood.* Arlington: Organization for Autism Research.

Davis, K. (2005). "Creating a Circle of Support." Indiana Resource Center for Autism, http://www.iidc.indiana.edu/?pageId=411.

Diament, M. (2009). "Autism Moms Have Stress Similar to Combat Soldiers." Disability Scoop, http://www.disabilityscoop.com/2009/11/10/autism-moms-stress/6121.

Donnellan, A. M., D. A. Hill, and M. E. Leary (2010). "Rethinking Autism: Implications of Sensory and Movement Differences." *Disability Studies Quarterly,* http://www.dsq-sds.org/article/view/1060/1225.

Donnellan, A. M., and M. Leary (1995). *Movement Differences and Diversity in Autism/Mental Retardation: Appreciating and Accommodating People with Communication and Behavior Challenges.* Chicago, Illinois: DRI Press.

Dutton, M. K. (2008). "Autistic Students Get Help Navigating College Life." *USA Today,* http://www.usatoday.com/news/education/2008-07-08-autistic-college_N.htm.

Etmanski, A. (2000). *A Good Life: For You and Your Relative with a Disability.* Vancouver, BC: Planned Lifetime Advocacy Network.

Falvey, M., M. Forest, J. Pearpoint, and R. Rosenberg (1997). *All My Life's a Circle.* Toronto, Ontario: Inclusion Press.

Fielden, C., J. Nolan, S. Norton, E. Higginbotham, J. Janses, and P. Flores-Carter (2006). "Catching the Wave from High School to College: A Guide to Transition." Grossmont College, http://www.grossmont.edu/dsps/transition/transition00_default.asp.

Foden, T. J. (2008). "Adults with ASD: The Spectrum." Kennedy Krieger Institute, http://www.iancommunity.org/cs/articles/adults_spectrum.

Foundation for Autism Support and Training (2011a). "What Is in a Life Plan for Adults with Autism Spectrum Disorder?" Life Planning, http://foundationforautismsupportandtraining.org/lifePlanningAdults.html.

—— (2011b). "Group Homes and Residential Support for People with Autism." Foundation for Autism Support and Training, http://foundationforautismsupportandtraining.org/groupHomes.html.

Frombonne, E. (2007). "Social Skills Training Helpful for Autistic Teens." *Journal of Autism and Developmental Disorders.*

Gerhardt, P. (2009). "Current State of Services for Adults with Autism: A Report to the Advancing Futures for Adults with Autism Think Tank." Organization for Autism Research.

Grandin, T., and K. Duffy (2008). *Developing Talents: Careers for Individuals with Asperger Syndrome and High-Functioning Autism.* Shawnee Mission, Kansas: Autism Asperger Publishing Company.

Griffin, C., and D. Hammis (2003). *Making Self-Employment Work for People with Disabilities.* Baltimore: Brookes Publishing Company.

Griffin, C., D. Hammis, and T. Geary (2007). *The Job Developers Handbook: Practical Tactics for Customized Employment.* Baltimore: Brookes Publishing Company.

Hamilton, J. (2010). "Students with Autism Learn How to Succeed at Work." National Public Radio, http://www.npr.org/templates/story/story.php?storyId=127831876&sc=emaf.html (June 14, 2010).

Harpur, J., M. Lawlor, and M. Fitzgerald (2004). *Succeeding in College with Asperger Syndrome: A Student Guide.* New York: Jessica Kingsley Publishers.

Hawkins, G. (2004). *How to Find Work That Works for People with Asperger's Syndrome.* London: Jessica Kingsley Publishers.

Henault, I. (2005). *Asperger's Syndrome and Sexuality: From Adolescence Through Adulthood.* London: Jessica Kingsley Publishers.

Heasley, S. (2011). "Autism Families Getting By on Loss." Disability Scoop, http://www.disabilityscoop.com/2011/05/12/autism-families-less/13084.html.

Hillier, A., T. Fish, P. Cloppert, and D. Q. Beversdorf (2007). "Outcomes of a Social and Vocational Skills Support Group for Adolescents and Young Adults on the Autism Spectrum." *Focus on Autism and Other Developmental Disabilities, 22,* 107–15.

Howlin, P. (2005). "Outcomes in Autism Spectrum Disorders." Chapter 7, *Handbook of Autism and Pervasive Developmental Disorders*, 3rd ed., F. Volkmar, A. Klin, R. Paul, and D. Cohen, eds. Hoboken, New Jersey: Wiley, 201–22.

Howlin, P., and P. Yate (1999). "The Potential Effectiveness of Social Skills Groups for Adults with Autism." *Autism,* 3: 299–307.

Hundley, M. (2011). "New Research: Asperger Syndrome and Depression." Suite 101, http://www.suite101.com/content/new-research-asperger-syndrome-and-depression-a379896.

Ken's Krew (2011). "Championing Ability . . . Enabling Success." Ken's Krew, http://kenskidsinc.org/index.html.

King, B. R. (2011). *Let's Relate on the Autism Spectrum: Strategies for Building Meaningful Relationships.* London: Jessica Kingsley Publications.

Knust-Potter, E. (2011). "Impressum/About Us." Circles of Support in India and Europe, http://www.cos-transnational.net/typo/index.php/impressum.html.

Krauss, M. W., M. M. Seltzer, and H. T. Jacobson (2005). "Adults with Autism Living at Home or in Non-Family Settings: Positive and Negative Aspects of Residential Status." *Journal of Intellectual Disability Research,* 49(2), 111–24.

Lagace, M. (2011). "The Surprising Right Fit for Software Testing—Executive Education Program." Boston: President and Fellows of Harvard College Harvard Business School.

Leary, M. R., and D. A. Hill (1996). "Moving On: Autism and Movement Disturbance." *Mental Retardation,* November, 39–53.

LeBaron, M. (2003). "Communication Tools for Understanding Cultural Differences." Beyond Intractability, http://www.beyondintractability.org.

Lieberman, L. (2005). *A "Stranger" Among Us: Hiring In-Home Supports for a Child with Autism Spectrum Disorders or Other Neurological Differences.* Shawnee Mission, Kansas: Autism Asperger Publishing Co.

Luecking, R., S. Fabian, and G. Tilson (2004). *Working Relationships: Creating Career Opportunities for Job Seekers with Disabilities Through Employer Partnerships.* Baltimore: Brookes Publishing Company.

Mandell, D., C. Walrath, D, Manteuffel, G. Sgro, and E. Pinto-Martin (2005). "The Prevalence and Correlates of Abuse Among Children with Autism Served in Comprehensive Community-Based Mental Health Settings." *Child Abuse & Neglect, 29,* 1359–72.

Meyer, R. (2001). *Asperger Syndrome Employment Workbook: An Employment Workbook for Adults with Asperger Syndrome.* London: Jessica Kingsley Publishers.

Mitra, M., V. Mouradian, M. Diamond (2011). "Sexual Violence Victimization Against Men with Disabilities." *American Journal of Preventative Medicine 41*(5), www.ajpmonline.org.

Nadworny, J. W. (2007). *The Special Needs Planning Guide: How to Prepare for Every Stage of Your Child's Life.* Baltimore: Paul H. Brookes Publishing Co.

Nayate, A., J. L. Bradshaw, and N. J. Rinehart (2005). "Autism and Asperger's Disorder: Are They Movement Disorders Involving the Cerebellum and/or Basal Ganglia." *Brain Research Bulletin,* October, 327–34.

Nerney, T. (2007). "Doing More with Less: Rethinking Long Term Care." Autism Society of Greater Cleveland, http://www.asgc.org/ed-self-determine.htm.

Newton, N., and A. Kaur (2007). "Stalking, and Social and Romantic Functioning Among Adolescents and Adults with Autism Spectrum Disorder Mark Stokes." Springer Science+Business Media, LLC.

Orsmond, G. I., M. W. Krauss, and M. M. Seltzer (2004). "Peer Relationships and Social and Recreational Activities Among Adolescents and Adults with Autism." *Journal of Autism and Developmental Disorders, 3,* 245–56.

Palmer, A. (2006). *Realizing the College Dream with Autism or Asperger's Syndrome: A Parent's Guide to Student Success.* Philadelphia: Jessica Kingsley Publishers.

Patton, A. (2010). "Space and Touch." *Communication Aspects of International Public Relations,* http://iml.jou.ufl.edu/projects/Spring02/Patton /spaceandtouch.

Peterson, M. (1997). "Building Caring Communities: Contributions of People with Disabilities." http://education.wayne.edu/wholeschooling/WS /WSPress/ArtBuildCare.html.

Rand, M., and J. Truman (2009). "Criminal Victimization." The U.S. Department of Justice, http://bjs.ojp.usdoj.gov/index.cfm?ty=pbdetail&iid=2217.

Renty, J. O., and H. Roeyers (2006). "Quality of Life in High-Functioning Adults with Autism Spectrum Disorder: The Predictive Value of Disability and Support Characteristics." *Autism, 10*(5), 511–24.

Riches, V. (2010). "Who Supports the Support Staff?" Centre for Disability Studies and the University of Sydney.

Robinson, R. (2011). *Autism Solutions: How to Create a Healthy and Meaningful Life for Your Child.* Buffalo: Harlequin.

Rudy, L. J. (2009a). "Finding the Right Home for Your Adult Child with Autism." About.com Guide, http://autism.about.com/od /adultsonthespectrum/a/housingehlert.htm.

—— (2007b). "Sexuality and Autism: Sex Education for Children and Teens with Autism." About.com Guide, http://autism.about.com/od/transition collegejobs/f/sexed.htm.

Samovar, L. A., R. E. Porter, and E. R. McDaniel (2009). *Intercultural Communication.* Boston: Wadsworth Cengage Learning.

Seltzer, M., and M. Krauss (2011). "Reflections from Adult Siblings Who Have a Brother or Sister with an Autism Spectrum Disorder." Strength For Caring, http://www.strengthforcaring.com/daily-care/caring-for -someone-with-autism/reflections-from-adult-siblings-who-have-a -brother-or-sister-with-an-autism-spectrum-disorder/.

Shute, N. (2009). "Teenagers with Autism: Want a Job?" *U.S. News,* http://health.usnews.com/health-news/family-health/brain-and -behavior/articles/2009/04/02/teenagers-with-autism-want-a-job?s _cid=related-links:TOP.

Simone, R. (2010). *Asperger's on the Job: Must-Have Advice for People with Asperger's or High Functioning Autism and Their Employers, Educators, and Advocate.* Arlington: Future Horizons.

Sicile-Kira, C. (2006a). *Adolescents on the Autism Spectrum: A Parent's Guide to the Cognitive, Social, Physical, and Transition Needs of Teenagers with Autism Spectrum Disorders.* New York: Penguin.

—— (2008b). *Autism Life Skills: From Communication and Safety to Self-Esteem and More: 10 Essential Abilities Every Child Deserves and Needs to Learn.* New York: Penguin.

—— (2004c). *Autism Spectrum Disorders: The Complete Guide to Understanding Autism, Asperger's Syndrome, Pervasive Development Disorder, and Other ASDs.* New York: Penguin.

—— (2010d). *41 Things to Know about Autism.* New York: Turner Publishing Co.

Smith, L. E., J. Hong, M. M. Seltzer, J. S. Greenberg, D. M. Almeida, and S. L. Bishop (2010). "Daily Experiences Among Mothers of Adolescents and Adults with Autism Spectrum Disorder." *Journal of Autism and Developmental Disorders, 40,* 167–78.

Smith, L. E., J. S. Greenberg, M. M. Seltzer, J. Hong, F. Floyd, and L. Abbeduto (2008). "Symptoms and Behavior Problems of Adolescents and Adults with Autism: Effects of Mother–Child Relationship Quality, Warmth, and Praise." *American Journal on Mental Retardation, 113,* 387–402.

Social Security Online (2011). "Plans to Achieve Self-Support (PASS)." Program Development and Research, http://www.ssa.gov/disability research/wi/pass.htm.

South Carolina Autism Society (2010). "Myths, Fables, Stories, Legends, Fiction and Misunderstandings." South Carolina Autism Society, http://www.scautism.org/myths.html.

Southwest Autism Research and Resource Center (2011). "Vocational/Life Skills Training." SARRC, http://www.autismcenter.org/Vocational .aspx.

Standifer, S. (2009). *Adult Autism & Employment: A Guide for Vocational Rehabilitation Professionals.* Disability Policy and Studies School of Health Professions, University of Missouri Health System.

Stanford, A. (2011). *Business for Aspies: 42 Best Practices for Using Asperger Syndrome Traits at Work Successfully.* London: Jessica Kingsley Publishers.

State Council on Developmental Disabilities (2003). "Disabilities: A Public Health Priority for the State of California." Protection and Advocacy Inc., www.scdd.ca.gov/Abuse_and_Neglect.pdf.

Stokes, S. (2010). "Developing Expressive Communication Skills for Non-Verbal Children with Autism." Special Education Services: Autism Strategies for Intervention and Success, http://www.specialed.us /autism/index2.htm.

Storey, K., and C. Miner (2011). *Systematic Instruction of Functional Skills for Students and Adults with Disabilities.* Springfield, Illinois: Charles C. Thomas Pub. Ltd.

Sullivan, R. C. (2007). "The National Crisis in Adult Services for Individuals with Autism, A Call to Action." Autism Society of America.

Swanbrow, D. (2009). "Study of Relationships Between Adult Children and Parents." *Medical News Today,* http://www.medicalnewstoday.com /releases/149047.php.

Tantam, D. (2000). "Psychological Disorder in Adolescents and Adults with Asperger Syndrome." The National Autistic Society, http://aut.sagepub .com/content/4/1/47.short?rss=1&ssource=mfc.

Tarnai, B., and P. S. Wolfe (2008). "Social Stories for Sexuality Education for Persons with Autism/Pervasive Developmental Disorder." *Sexuality and Disability, 26,* 29–36.

Turner-Brown, L. M., T. D. Perry, G. S. Dichter, J. W. Bodfish, and D. L. Penn (2008). "Brief Report: Feasibility of Social Cognition and Interaction Training for Adults with High Functioning Autism." *Journal of Autism and Developmental Disorders, 38,* 1777–84.

United Press International, Inc. (2011). "Virtual Conversation Aids Autistic Adults." United Press International, Inc., http://www.upi.com /Health_News/2011/03/19/Virtual-conversation-aids autistic-adults /UPI-77161300578675/.

University of Toronto (1999). "An Overview of the Quality of Life Project." University of Toronto, Quality of Life Research Unit, http://www .utoronto.ca/qol/unit.htm.

Wareham, J., and T. Sonne (2008). *Harnessing the Power of Autism Spectrum Disorder (Innovations Case Narrative: Specialisterne).* Cambridge, Massachusetts: MIT Press.

Web MD LCC (2010). "History of Autism." WebMD LCC, http://www .webmd.com/brain/autism/history-of-autism.

Wehman, P., et al. (2009). *Autism and the Transition to Adulthood: Success Beyond the Classroom.* Baltimore: Paul H. Brookes Publishing Company.

Wetherow, D., and F. Wetherow (2004). "Introduction to Microboards." Microboards and Microboard Association Design, Development and Implementation, http://www.communityworks.info/articles/microboard .htm.

Williams, G., and A. Palmer (2011). "Preparing for College: Tips for Students with HFA/Asperger's Syndrome." The University of Northern Carolina at Chapel Hill School of Medicine, http://teacch.com /educational-approaches/preparing-for-college-tips-for-students-with -hfa-aspergers-syndrome-new-gladys-williams-and-ann-palmer.

Wolf, L. E. (2009). *A Guide for College Personnel.* Shawnee Mission, Kansas: Autism Asperger Publishing Company.

Zaks, Z. (2006). *Life and Love: Positive Strategies for Autistic Adults.* Shawnee Mission, Kansas: Autism Asperger Publishing Company.

ABOUT THE AUTHORS

Chantal Sicile-Kira is the founder of AutismCollege.com, which provides practical training and conferences to parents and educators. A former TV producer based in France, she is an award-winning author, columnist, and speaker on autism. Her first experience with autism was teaching young adults the skills they needed to be deinstitutionalized from a California state hospital. Chantal was appointed by the California Senate Select Committee on Autism & Related Disorders to serve as Co-Chair, South Counties Autism Regional Taskforce, and on the Transitional Services & Supports Taskforce of the California Legislative Blue Ribbon Commission on Autism. Her other books are *Autism Spectrum Disorders, Adolescents on the Autism Spectrum, Autism Life Skills,* and *41 Things to Know About Autism.* Sicile-Kira writes for HuffingtonPost.com and PsychologyToday.com. Her story has been covered by a wide variety of media, including NPR, PBS, MTV, the *Chicago Tribune, Newsweek,* and Fox News. For more information, visit chantalsicilekira.com.

Jeremy Sicile-Kira was diagnosed as severely autistic when he was born in 1989. In 2010, he gave a commencement speech at his high school graduation. Jeremy is a college student and an advocate who writes and presents on autism, disability awareness, and overcoming challenges. Jeremy was featured in *Newsweek,* and in 2007 Jeremy was on MTV's *True Life* in the episode "I Have Autism," which won a Voice Award. For more information, visit jeremysicilekira.com. Follow Jeremy on Google+ and Twitter @jeremyisms.

JOIN THE CONVERSATION

We can create positive change by discussing ideas, sharing information, and creating connections. Join the conversation at Autism College.com.

INDEX